T0317687

RECONSTRUCTING CONTRACTS

RECONSTRUCTING CONTRACTS

DOUGLAS G. BAIRD

Harvard University Press

Cambridge, Massachusetts

London, England

2013

Copyright © 2013 by the President and Fellows of Harvard College
All rights reserved
Printed in the United States of America

Library of Congress Cataloging-in-Publication Data

Baird, Douglas G., 1953–
Reconstructing contracts / Douglas G. Baird.
p. cm.
Includes bibliographical references and index.
ISBN 978-0-674-07248-0 (alk. paper)
1. Contracts—United States. 2. Contracts—Great Britain. I. Title.
KF801.B35 2013
346.7302'2—dc23   2012038116

For Julie and Sam

CONTENTS

Preface   *ix*

Introduction: The Young Astronomer   *1*

1 Objective Intent   *9*

2 The Bargained-for Exchange   *25*

3 Holmes's Bad Man   *46*

4 The Expectation Damages Principle and
   Its Limits   *57*

5 Terms of Engagement   *78*

6 Mistake, Excuse, and Implicit Terms   *96*

7 Duress and the Availability of the
   Legal Remedy   *111*

8 Fine Print: Contracts in Mass Markets   *123*

   Epilogue: The Boundaries of Contract   *147*

   Notes   *153*
   Index   *167*

PREFACE

This volume brings together some of the thinking I have done about contract law over the past two decades. This project began with the 1992 Katz Lecture at the University of Chicago Law School. It was also called "Reconstructing Contracts." That talk contained the seed for what is now the second chapter of this book. Ideas from other work can be found throughout each of the chapters. This book does not set out the essential doctrines of contract law. Marvin Chirelstein, Eric Posner, and others have already done this task far more ably than I could. My attempt has been rather to reflect on the fundamental principles of contracts. In particular, my ambition is to assess where we stand today in an enterprise that Oliver Wendell Holmes began in 1880 when he gave his lectures on the common law and sought, among other things, to set out a few core ideas that unite the law of contracts.

When I was in law school, the conventional wisdom was that Holmes's enterprise was a pipe dream. Contract law itself did not have metes and bounds that could be laid out neatly. If this book has any general theme, it is that this view is fundamentally wrong. The Anglo-American law of contract does organize itself around a handful of straightforward ideas. They are not immutable and universal laws in the fashion of those of Newton or Einstein, but they are useful principles nevertheless.

Far from presenting a view of contract law that is distinctively my own, these essays reflect what I have learned from the extraordinary contracts scholars whose orbits have crossed mine. These begin with Thomas Jackson and Robert Scott. I had the great privilege of working with both while a law student. Later came many others. Most prominent among them is Richard Posner, whose influence permeates every essay. They also include my colleagues Lisa Bernstein, Ronald Coase, Richard Craswell,

Frank Easterbrook, Richard Epstein, Robert Gordon, Stanley Henderson, Cass Sunstein, and the late Brian Simpson. Each uncovered foundational ideas reflected in this book. There are many other scholars whose work I have studied and enjoyed. I am deeply indebted to all of them and hope this book can be understood as a celebration of their work, even when seen through the somewhat imperfect lens I bring to it.

RECONSTRUCTING CONTRACTS

Introduction

The Young Astronomer

Courts enforce the promises one merchant makes to another according to their terms. This proposition is nearly always true in virtually every country and every legal system in the world. But this leaves much unsettled. Two merchants exchange multiple communications with one another. How do courts decide when and if they have entered into a binding contract? Contingencies can arise that no one thought about. When gaps are left in an agreement, how should courts fill them in? And what exactly does it mean to say that a court will enforce a promise? Will the court order performance, impose a fine, or order the payment of damages? If the court orders the payment of damages, how will these be measured? It is equally true that, in contrast to promises made in the marketplace, courts everywhere refuse to enforce casual promises made in a social setting. How exactly is the line drawn between the two?

The answers to these questions again tend to be the same across legal systems throughout the world. Many disputes, indeed the vast majority of them, are easily resolved and will be decided the same regardless of the legal system. But lawyers, at least the good ones, are not hired to win easy cases, and the hard cases are not always decided identically. Even when they are, the path that brings the judge to a certain outcome is not the same. Each legal system organizes itself differently. The contract law of each is a distinct language. To speak it well, one must understand its unique cadences as well as its vocabulary and grammar.

At the start of the Anglo-American legal tradition, a lawsuit began as a petition to the Crown. A citizen who was the victim of a breach of promise asked the Crown to use the power of the state—including force if necessary—to put matters right. The Crown did not grant relief as a matter of course. The power of the state would not come to the aid of a citizen merely because a promise had been broken. Using force to compel one citizen to right a wrong allegedly done to another was a serious business. It would not be done without good reason, and it would not be done arbitrarily. The citizen had to explain what it was about the broken promise in question that made it worthy of the Crown's attention. To do this, the citizen's job was to explain why this case was like the others before in which relief had been granted. Authority lay in precedent.

There are other ways of proceeding. Some legal systems—such as those in Europe and Japan—begin with a set of general principles and require judges to reason from them when deciding any particular dispute. But the Anglo-American system did not start in this fashion, and it has not changed. Our legal system still rests on a vast body of decided cases from which general principles must be extracted. Anglo-American lawyers face the challenge of locating a given set of facts among the vast forest of cases that have been decided before. From the tens of thousands of reported decisions, they must find those that are closest. Legal scholars have long sought to identify from all these cases a handful that is representative. By giving lawyers a few landmarks, scholars help them find their bearings.

The modern study of contract law begins properly with Christopher Columbus Langdell's appointment to the deanship of the Harvard Law School in 1871. He instituted the case method of legal instruction, and he set the example for others with his course on contracts. Instead of a book that set forth principles in the abstract, his contracts book provided a representative set of decided cases. Students learned the law by reading them closely. Langdell believed that fundamental principles were embedded in the cases he selected. Just as the immutable laws that governed the natural world could be discovered through close observation of a few phenomena, the essential features of contract law could be found in these judicial opinions.

Oliver Wendell Holmes began his own intense study of the law at about the same time that Langdell brought his revolution to the Harvard Law School. He too looked for the core principles of the common law and more or less replicated Langdell's effort to identify the central principles of contract. A novel written at the time portrays a thinly disguised Holmes as he goes about this task. He is the Young Astronomer, a man obsessed with fixing his attention to the thousands of stars in the heavens and making sense of them.[1]

In contrast to Langdell, Holmes doubted that immutable laws of science governed the movement of the legal heavens. Laws reflect in some measure the circumstances that brought them into being:

> [W]hile, on the one hand, there are a great many rules which are quite sufficiently accounted for by their manifest good sense, on the other, there are some which can only be understood by reference to the infancy of procedure among the German tribes, or to the social condition of Rome under the Decemvirs.[2]

Legal rules are grounded in history and are path dependent.

> [J]ust as the clavicle in the cat only tells of the existence of some earlier creature to which a collarbone was useful, precedents survive in the law long after the use they once served is at an end, and the reason for them has been forgotten. The result of following them must often be failure and confusion from the merely logical point of view.[3]

Nevertheless, Holmes shared with Langdell the belief that one could identify a relatively simple set of patterns that could explain how judges behaved. He too believed that careful study of a handful of paradigmatic cases could capture the basic principles a lawyer needed in order to understand the peculiar rhythms and harmonies of the common law.

For Holmes, the law of contract revolved around three central ideas. First, objective criteria controlled the formation of a contract. A subjective meeting of the minds was not the benchmark. There is instead an objective test that tells us whether, at any moment, you are contractually bound or not. Second, only those promises that are part of a bargained-for exchange are legally enforceable. A promise is legally enforceable only if it is given in exchange for something else, such as another promise. Third, when you break a legally enforceable promise, you are required to pay compensatory damages—that amount of money that will put the innocent party in the same position that party would have been in had the promise been kept.

Writing some forty years ago, Grant Gilmore surveyed the landscape of decided contract cases and concluded that the coherence that Holmes had tried to impart with these principles had fallen apart. He called his masterful account of the law of contracts *Death of Contract*. He observed:

> The instinctive hope of the great system-builders was, no doubt, that the future development of the law could be, if not controlled, at least channeled in an orderly and rational fashion. That hope has proved, in our century of war and revolution, delusive. The systems have come unstuck and we see, presently, no way of gluing them back together again.[4]

The idea that contractual liability has a yes/no, on/off character is much more troubling than Holmes and others understood. Consider the following case.[5] A worker goes to her boss a week after her written contract expires. The worker says that if her contract is not going to be renewed, she needs to know. Another firm has offered her a job at the same salary. She would prefer to stay, but if she is not given a contract for the next year, she will leave. Her boss tells her, "You have nothing to worry about. Go back to your job. We like the work you are doing." The boss is encouraging but does not explicitly use any of the ordinary words of contracting.

Someone committed to Holmes's position is in an awkward spot. If you believe this conduct is insufficient to form a contract, then the boss is free to fire the worker several months later after the worker has given up the chance to move elsewhere. But if you think there is a contract, you face another unattractive possibility.

A minute after the exchange, the boss realizes that she might have been misunderstood. She catches up with the worker and says, "Look, it occurs to me that you may have misunderstood. I cannot agree to bind the company to a contract now. You are going to have to hang in limbo. I hope you stay, but if you don't like it, then I'm afraid you will have to take the other job." If you really think that the previous exchange formed a contract, the worker could say, "Sorry, boss. It is too late. You are committed to having me around for another year." The boss is liable, regardless of whether the worker has relied in any way on the conversation that took place a minute before.

For many who thought deeply about contracts in the last half of the twentieth century, it was more sensible to view a contract as merely another species of civil obligation. We assess the conduct of the parties and establish relative culpability as we do with other sorts of injury. If the worker has not relied on the promise, damages should not be awarded.

If she has, then she should be made whole, but only to the extent she has reasonably relied. Justice requires no more.

The classical view of contract, from this perspective, made little sense. The liability of one person to another should not turn sharply on a single, discontinuous moment. There should not be an instantaneous transition from a world of no liability to a world in which you were liable to the extent of the full value of the promise. Nor should promising behavior give rise to legal liability only when it was part of a bargained-for exchange. It makes far more sense to hold people to their words as a general matter to the extent that others reasonably rely on them.

Moreover, one must doubt the positive account that Holmes and Langdell offer. Once we begin to question the classical principles, we start to discover cases that do not fit in the traditional paradigm. There are, for example, many instances in which courts enforce promises reasonably relied upon even when there is no bargained-for exchange. Once one finds enough of these cases, Holmes's principles no longer provide a road map. The classical view of contract falls apart. And once one accepts this general notion that individuals are responsible for their words that are reasonably relied upon, there is little left of Holmes's core principles. Contractual liability is no longer an on/off objective proposition limited to bargained-for exchanges and generating liability for full-expectation damages. Instead, it is merely a species of civil liability. It is subsumed within tort law. We face the death of contract.

In the forty years since *Death of Contract,* contract has yet to morph into a species of tort. The revolutionary doctrines of the first half of the twentieth century, such as promissory estoppel, have had only modest and limited scope in practice. The core principles that Holmes put forward are still very much with us, but their logic and limits are now much better understood.

We share the view of the legal realists that some rules are arbitrary, but we no longer see such formality as a vice. There is a virtue in having a realm of contract, apart from ordinary civil liability, that is demarcated by clear rules. We have concluded that these rules work well enough. The debate is not much over whether formal rules are arbitrary. Instead, it is over whether the formal rules we have work as well as they might or whether others might work better.

The worker would like to know where she stands. In a world in which everything turns on reliance, we shall not know if her job is assured until there has been a jury trial. The boss would like to be in a world where she does not have to worry about whether she has entered into a contract every time she puts off an employee. The world is a better place if the process of creating a legally enforceable contract is subject to a clear set of conventions.

Consider the following legal rule: no deal unless there is sealing wax. Until the boss signs, seals, and delivers a new contract, the firm can get off the hook. Assume that parties know that this was the legal rule. If parties know the legal rule and if it is the legal rule that largely determines the behavior of the parties, everyone would know where they stand. If the boss is evasive, the worker can respond, "Look, I do not want to be a pest, but our hands are tied by this legal rule. I need to have the certainty of having a job for another year, and I can't have it if you do not get out the sealing wax. You have to make up your mind: Do you want me or not? If you tell me simply that I am all right or that my job is secure, that is just as good as telling me there is no deal. Anything short of sealing wax means that you have not entered into the contract with me."

This sort of formal legal rule tells all the players where they stand. It does not allow for ambiguity. The worker either gets the contract, or she is still an employee at will, someone who can be dismissed for any reason or no reason at all. But there is a dark side of formal rules as well. In a world in which you have to use sealing wax, "Don't worry, it's OK" means the same as "Have a nice day." Formal rules work only to the extent that people know them and pay attention to them, and this will not always happen.

There is no single answer to the question of whether a formal legal rule makes sense in any environment. Often formalities create more trouble than they are worth. But instead of thinking of formal legal rules as being out of step with the underlying reality, we are now inclined to see how they can be tools that parties can fashion for their own purposes. Contract law is essentially an empty vessel that allows parties to organize their affairs in a way that makes them better off.

We no longer think of the specific rules of contract law, such as expectation damages, as capturing some set of values immanent in the grand scheme of things. They make sense because they serve a useful purpose. In the case of expectation damages, for example, the legal rule forces each of the parties to internalize the costs that their breach will impose on the other. It is not the only rule parties might pick, but it is a sensible one. Given that parties cannot spell out all the terms of their contract, it is useful to have contract law provide terms that work for most parties most of the time.

Much of the work of contract law lies in fleshing out the bargain that parties strike between themselves. As noted at the chapter's opening, courts will enforce the bargains of merchants according to their terms. Problems arise when the terms are not clear or, more often, incomplete. Much of contract law simply fills in gaps that apply when the parties are silent. Contract law, in other words, consists largely of default rules. Parties are free to vary them if they choose, and there is no virtue in requiring parties to adopt one set of contract terms rather than another.

This heuristic, like every other, has its limitations. Parties never have all the time and the money in the world. Asking what bargain parties would strike if bargaining were easy misses fundamental features of our world. Nevertheless, asking what sort of deal two merchants would reach if they could bargain over a term explicitly is nearly always a good starting place. If you press for a rule that is something other than what you think most people would want if they thought about it, you should offer some explanation.

This view of contract law as a set of default rules has become part of the mainstream in recent years, but it is hardly new. It can be seen at work in Holmes's own contract opinions. The law should endeavor to impose on a party those contract terms "which it fairly may be presumed he would have assented to if they had been presented to his mind."[6]

In the first four chapters of this book, I examine the traditional principles that Holmes thought foundational to the law of contract, and then I review the contemporary understanding of them. In Chapter 1, I examine the idea that a contract does not require a subjective meeting of the minds. Instead, we use an objective benchmark to determine whether two parties have reached an agreement with each other. As has been the custom in contract classes for more than a century, the classic case of *Raffles v. Wichelhaus* provides the point of entry. Chapter 2 explores the traditional idea that a legally enforceable contract comes into being only when there is a bargained-for exchange. Another canonical case, *Hamer v. Sidway*, is again the focal point of the discussion. The next two chapters look at the idea that courts enforce promises by requiring the payment of money damages. Chapter 3 focuses on Holmes's idea that one can understand what courts are doing by treating the promisor's obligation as an option to pay money damages in the event she does not perform.

Chapter 4 explores the expectation damages principle, the idea that the damages awarded for breach of contract should equal the amount sufficient to put the promisee in the same position she would have been in had the promise been kept.

The next three chapters examine the rules against which parties negotiate their original bargain or seek to modify it. In Chapter 5, I explore the background understanding the law imparts to commercial dealing between parties, both in the good faith duties they assume and their disclosure obligations to one another. Chapter 6 explores the doctrines of excuse and mistake, while Chapter 7 looks at the doctrine of duress and the challenge of distinguishing mutually beneficial renegotiation in light of changed circumstances from advantage taking. In Chapter 8, I examine how the law of contract operates in the marketplace where standardized terms are the norm, and there is none of the one-on-one bargaining between *A* and *B* that is the stuff of the traditional law school hypothetical. In a brief Epilogue, I take stock of where we stand today in the Holmesian enterprise of demarcating the boundaries of contract law.

1

Objective Intent

William Winter Raffles was a cotton broker in Liverpool in the middle of the nineteenth century.[1] His agents acquired cotton for him abroad, and he sold it in England, either to textile mills directly or to others who might hold it and try to resell it at a profit. In January 1863, Raffles was trying to sell 125 bales of cotton on a ship that had just left Bombay and would arrive in Liverpool in April. He found Daniel Wichelhaus, a cotton speculator. He agreed to give him 125 bales of cotton, roughly twenty-five tons, "to arrive ex 'Peerless' from Bombay," and in return Wichelhaus agreed to pay 17¼d a pound.

The price for cotton was particularly volatile that January. Most southern ports in the United States were blockaded. The Union's success at the Battle of Antietam and the resolve Lincoln showed in issuing the Emancipation Proclamation (and the House in affirming it) suggested that the war would continue for a long time, and the market for cotton would remain uncertain. The price fell somewhat and remained unstable. Cotton sold for 16¼d in February and then rose to 16¾d in April.

When the cotton arrived in April, Raffles demanded that Wichelhaus honor his promise to buy it, but Wichelhaus refused. He said there had been a misunderstanding. Raffles tendered Wichelhaus cotton from a ship called *Peerless* that had left Bombay in December, while Wichelhaus thought he was being offered cotton from a ship called *Peerless* that had left in October. Because each was thinking about cotton on different ships, Wichelhaus argued that they never had a deal with each other.

Raffles argued that it made no difference whether they had been thinking of different ships. Raffles produced the cotton in the amount and grade he promised and that was all that mattered. The identity of the ship was not relevant to the bargain they struck. "Peerless" was a common name for a

9

ship during this period. In addition to the two involved in this case, there were seven other British sailing vessels registered under that name. That Wichelhaus had thought the cotton was on a different ship was neither here nor there. Raffles had cotton on only one of the ships called *Peerless*.

Raffles reduced the dispute to this point alone by demurring to Wichelhaus's pleading. The contemporary equivalent under the *Federal Rules of Civil Procedure* is a motion for judgment on the pleadings. Today Raffles would be able to continue the litigation even if he lost a motion for judgment on the pleadings. At the time, however, a party that lost a demurrer lost the entire case. Raffles essentially was saying, "So what? Who cares?" Even if what Wichelhaus said was true, it did not make the slightest bit of difference. The bargain was over the cotton.

An example illustrates the essence of Raffles's argument. You visit me and see both of the red Porsches that I own. I point to one and explain that it is my city Porsche. The other is my country Porsche, which I use mostly on weekends. You ask how I protect them against the weather, and I explain that I keep my city Porsche in the Michigan Street Garage, which is close to where I live during the week, and I keep my country Porsche in the California Street Garage, which is only a block from my country home. As it happens, there are two California Street Garages. One is in Naperville, which is the one I use. The other is in Libertyville. I do not live in Libertyville, and I do not park my Porsche in a garage there. Indeed, I have never been to Libertyville.

We meet later and you express an interest in buying one of my cars. I agree to sell you the one stored in the California Street Garage. I will deliver it to your house on Saturday. When I refer to the California Street Garage, you might think I am talking about the California Street Garage in Libertyville. After all, you do not know the location of my country home. But this makes no difference. We have a contract for a particular Porsche, and we both know which one it is. If I had red Porsches in each of the California Street Garages, you might have something to complain about. (You might have thought you were buying one Porsche, and I thought I was selling another.) But that is not the case here. "California Street Garage" uniquely identifies which of my Porsches we are talking about, no matter how many California Street Garages there are. The only work that "California Street Garage" is doing in the contract is distinguishing my country Porsche from my city Porsche. Otherwise, the garage in which the car is parked makes no difference. It is not material to our bargain.

I have to tender a particular Porsche; Raffles has to tender the specified cotton. I mention a garage; Raffles names a ship. It would matter that there were two California Street Garages if I had Porsches in both or that there were two ships called *Peerless* if Raffles had cotton on both. But I have only one Porsche in a garage on California Street, and it is in the garage in Napierville, and Raffles has cotton only on a ship called *Peerless,* and it is the December *Peerless.* We never need to talk about the garage in Libertyville or the second *Peerless.*

The court, however, did not buy the argument that the identity of the ship was immaterial. Indeed, the judges decided in favor of Wichelhaus after hearing only a few words of his lawyer's argument. As Gilmore explained, Raffles lost because "the judges . . . believed that the identity of the carrying ship was important—a true condition of the contract." In this, Gilmore had "no doubt" but that the judges were mistaken. Raffles's understanding of the relevance of the name of the ship was the correct one. The contract term "to arrive ex Peerless"

> meant only that "if the vessel is lost on the voyage, the contract is to be at an end" (that is, the seller would bear the loss but the buyer would have no claim for damages for non-delivery). In commercial understanding, that is exactly what the terms mean today and there is no reason to believe that they meant anything else a hundred years ago.[2]

As it happens, Gilmore was mistaken. A decade after *Death of Contract,* Brian Simpson took a close look at the nineteenth-century Liverpool cotton market and discovered that the name of the ship in such contracts "to arrive" served a distinct function over and above identifying goods in the event they were destroyed.

Today speculators like Wichelhaus can bet on the price of cotton by entering into a futures contract. The futures market for cotton did not exist in 1863. To speculate on the price of cotton, one had to buy and sell the physical commodity. It was possible to hold cotton, of course, but storing it was expensive. A better alternative was to buy or sell cotton that was en route. A ship took four months to sail from Bombay to Liverpool, but it took only a month for news of its departure from Bombay to reach Liverpool. While it was at sea, identifiable lots of cotton could be bought and sold. By entering into a "contract to arrive," you could gamble on the future price of cotton without having to incur the expense of storing it. In a contract such as the one involved in *Raffles,* a one-penny change in the price of cotton represented a £200 gain or loss.

The exact date any particular ship would arrive in port was not clear in advance. Hence, the contracts referred to the ships rather than a specific time for delivery. A contract involving the October *Peerless* was as close as you could come to a futures contract for February cotton, and a contract involving the December *Peerless* was for April cotton. In promising in January to buy cotton "ex *Peerless*," Wichelhaus believed he was buying cotton for delivery the next month, and in promising to sell cotton "ex *Peerless*," Raffles believed he was selling cotton in three months.

Seen from this perspective, it makes a considerable difference which ship contained the cotton. Someone who wants cotton delivered in February is not necessarily interested in buying cotton that will arrive only in April. Such a buyer may himself have an obligation to deliver cotton to someone else in February. Cotton on the October *Peerless* hedges bets in a way that cotton on the December *Peerless* does not.

At the time Raffles and Wichelhaus entered into their contract, the futures price of February cotton and April cotton might have been about the same. Although there might be some differences because the market demand may be cyclical and storage is costly, in a market that is not well developed, the forward price for February and April cotton might be about the same as the spot price in January. But even if the price is the same, the contracts are not. An obligation to deliver cotton in February, when cotton sells at one price, is different from the obligation to deliver cotton in April, when it sells at a different price. Moreover, to beat back the demurrer, Wichelhaus needed to show only that the difference might matter—that one could not assume the differences were immaterial from the face of the pleadings alone.

As noted, the price of cotton declined significantly between the time of the contract and the time the first *Peerless* arrived in Liverpool. There was a full penny per pound difference between the contract price and the market price in February. Because Raffles failed to act at all when the first ship arrived, even though doing so would have profited him handsomely, he likely always intended to deliver cotton in April and had intended the December *Peerless* rather than the October *Peerless*. He would be unlikely to have cotton of the contract description on both ships.

Wichelhaus's silence after Raffles's failure to deliver may reflect his reluctance to acknowledge a losing deal. If, as he claimed, Wichelhaus had wanted cotton in February and had therefore intended the October *Peerless*, he would have expected Raffles to call and tender delivery of cotton from the ship that docked in February. But Wichelhaus had no reason to encourage Raffles to perform under a contract when it no longer benefited him. He was entitled to remain silent. When the second ship

Peerless arrived in April and Raffles demanded payment, Wichelhaus, if he had always expected cotton on the February ship and had known nothing of the April ship, would likely have behaved much as he did. He had a losing contract for February cotton, but Raffles had never claimed his rights under that contract. And by April, Raffles was too late. One cannot meet a futures contract for February delivery with April delivery.

It is possible that Wichelhaus knew about the two ships by February and was trying to have it both ways. If the price of cotton remained below the contract price, he could, as he did, use the ambiguity in the contract to let himself off the hook. And if the price rose again above the contract price by April, he could have insisted that he had wanted cotton on the December *Peerless* all along and hold Raffles to what would now be for him a winning contract. It seems likely, however, that Wichelhaus at the outset had thought he was buying cotton that was to arrive in February. If he had not, Raffles would not have allowed the case to turn on the legal question of whether an enforceable contract had been formed.

Of course, not all ambiguities matter, as our example with the Porsche suggests. But to the extent that the name of the ship is a proxy for the delivery date, the difference between two different types of futures contracts is not something that can be glossed over.

The court found that the ambiguity of which *Peerless* was intended was dispositive. Although the court did not issue an opinion, it seemed to hold that in order for a contract to come into being, the minds of the parties must meet, at least with respect to all the material elements of the bargain. There has to be consent for a contract to be formed. There could be no contract in *Raffles* because, in the words of Wichelhaus's lawyer, there was no "consensus ad idem." Because each was thinking of a different ship and the identity of the ship mattered, there was no deal.

The debate that emerged out of this case was whether a subjective meeting of the minds on all material points was necessary for a contract to be formed at common law. At the time *Raffles* was decided, the theoretical foundations of contract law were unclear. Blackstone's *Commentaries* was the first book in every American lawyer's library in the eighteenth century. Blackstone tried to make the common law of England coherent, but he provided little help when it came to identifying the central principles of contract law.

No one ever accused Blackstone of being a deep thinker. He glorified the common law, but he had no philosophical intuitions and little historical sense. More to the point, the Industrial Revolution was only just beginning, and the law merchant had not been completely integrated into the common law. He was worried about the problems that arise in a largely land-based economy. He had little to say about contracts or indeed, about commercial law.

Contract law was not recognized as a separate subject until well into the nineteenth century. When people started to think seriously about the law of contracts, the rules of pleading were on their way out, and they no longer provided the conceptual framework for thinking about contracts. In seeking a framework, those in England first looked to thinkers on the Continent such as Savigny, who were steeped in Roman law and the civil law tradition.

One of the central ideas of Savigny's theory of contracts was that a subjective meeting of the minds was essential. In his discussion of Roman law, Savigny noted that there were some kinds of obligations that arose simply because the parties had engaged in a particular legal ritual. There were other obligations, however, that were enforced simply by virtue of consent. It was the existence of the meeting of the minds of the two parties itself that made the obligation enforceable. The legal obligation could arise only from "a union of several wills to a single, whole, and undivided will."[3] Savigny was understood to make this into a normative as well as a positive proposition. A contractual obligation should not exist if both parties did not will it. Before a contract became legally enforceable, the minds of the two parties had to meet. Unless they were in subjective agreement on all the issues that mattered, there could be no enforceable contract.

To the extent that Holmes had an agenda, it was to separate the study of the common law from the intellectual superstructure imposed by European thinkers like Savigny. A way to do this was to insist that it was independent of Roman law. In particular, Holmes sought to show that the contractual obligations at common law were not based on the will of the parties. Contracts are formed according to objective criteria, rather than the subjective intent of the parties. A binding contract on a given set of terms might exist even if one of the parties did not subjectively intend to enter such a contract.

The Young Astronomer, of course, cannot describe the stars as he wishes them to be. Holmes was heavily imbued with the spirit of pragmatism that pervaded his intellectual circle in Boston. He was attempting an account of the law not as it should be but rather the law as it was. The principles he described were to be assessed, in the words of pragmatists

Charles Sanders Pierce and William James, by their "cash value," the way in which they accurately captured what courts did.[4] Given this, how then could one explain *Raffles?*

Holmes rejected the idea that *Raffles* stood for the proposition that a subjective meeting of the minds was necessary. By his account, *Raffles* embraced an objective view of contractual obligation. What Raffles and Wichelhaus were thinking was irrelevant. They never reached a deal because they spoke past each other:

> The law has nothing to do with the actual state of the parties' minds. In contract, as elsewhere, it must go by externals, and judge parties by their conduct. If there had been but one "Peerless," and the defendant had said "Peerless" by mistake, meaning "Peri," he would have been bound. The true ground of the decision was not that each party meant a different thing from the other, . . . but that each said a different thing. The plaintiff offered one thing, the defendant expressed his assent to another.[5]

A case could arise in which parties thought about different ships and there was a binding contract nevertheless. It just happened that *Raffles* was not such a case. Measured by objective standards, each said something different.

Gilmore found this unconvincing. Raffles and Wichelhaus both said "Peerless." You could not argue that the parties said different things when they both used exactly the same words:

> Even for Holmes this was an extraordinary tour de force. . . . The magician who could "objectify" *Raffles v. Wichelhaus* . . . could, the need arising, objectify anything.[6]

But Gilmore was not giving Holmes enough credit.

You and I enter into a contract, and I promise to use Sam to provide IT support for the job. I am referring to the person named "Sam" whom I always use to provide IT support on my jobs. Most people who do business with me know the Sam to whom I am referring. Most do not need me to provide a last name nor do they expect me to. If someone happens to be uncertain about the person to whom I am referring, that person needs to ask. I am not required to be infinitely precise in the language I use. It just has to be good enough for most people to know what I am talking about.

Confusion, of course, can arise. Language is imperfect. Let us imagine that you know someone else who commonly provides IT support also named Sam. You have never heard of my Sam, and I have never heard of yours. You ask me to use "Sam" on the job and I agree. We are each thinking of different Sams. Neither one of us has tried to deceive the other. We are both using the same word, but we are referring to two different people. Those who know me best will think that the contract refers to my Sam, and those who know you best will think that the contract refers to your Sam. Those who know both of us may see that there is an ambiguity. We both use the same word, but objectively it has two different meanings.

What matters is the accepted convention for proper names. Each of us is entitled to rely on the link that we make between a proper noun and the person or object we associate with it. I can talk about my friend Sam and expect you to know to whom I am referring. If you are not sure, you need to ask. The same convention does not apply to ordinary nouns. I cannot use the word "pepper" when I mean "salt" and then later argue that there was never a meeting of the minds. If a merchant enters into a contract for "pepper" while genuinely thinking "salt," she will still be bound to deliver pepper. The words she actually spoke, as defined in the relevant lexicon, bind her regardless of what she subjectively believes.

This seems to capture Holmes's thinking about *Raffles*. As Holmes explains:

> A proper name, when used in business or in pleading, means one individual thing, and no other, as every one knows, and therefore one to whom such a name is used must find out at his peril what the object designated is. If there are no circumstances which make the use deceptive on either side, each is entitled to insist on the meaning favorable to him for the word as used by him, and neither is entitled to insist on that meaning for the word as used by the other.[7]

Consider what would we do if Raffles had actually said, "I will sell you cotton on the December *Peerless*," and Wichelhaus said, "I will buy cotton on the October *Peerless*." Measured objectively, the parties said two different things and never reached agreement with each other. We would conclude that there was no contract. The actual case is the same once we find that each is entitled to refer to the ship that he knows as *Peerless*.

From an objective point of view, the word "Peerless" means one thing when Raffles uses the word and another when Wichelhaus uses it. The world would be a better place if language were not so imprecise, but it is a failure of language in the objective sense. We can acknowledge such imprecision without believing that two individuals can be bound only if each thinks the same thing at the same time. Objectively measured, Raffles and Wichelhaus were talking about two different ships. They said two different things. We are bound by our words, not by our private thoughts, but we still need to determine what our words mean.

People communicate through a common language, and commerce depends on the use of this common language. Merchants need to be able to take what they say to each other at face value. You are required to use a common language. When you say "salt," I am entitled to hold you responsible for salt, regardless of what you were actually thinking about. Learned Hand captured this point in a vivid metaphor some years later:

> A contract has, strictly speaking, nothing to do with the personal, or individual, intent of the parties. A contract is an obligation attached by the mere force of law to certain acts of the parties, usually words, which ordinarily accompany and represent a known intent. If, however, it were proved by twenty bishops that either party, when he used the words, intended something else than the usual meaning which the law imposes upon them, he would still be held.[8]

Holmes's objective theory of contractual intent has taken hold and has not been seriously contested for more than a century. Although it may have seemed revolutionary in academic circles at the time of Holmes, it became a fixture in the modern understanding of the law in large part because it comports so well with how lawyers and judges approached such problems.

Indeed, it was a practicing lawyer who introduced *Raffles* to the canon, and his account is, in large measure, an objective one. Judah P. Benjamin was a prominent leader of the Confederacy who reinvented himself as an English barrister after he was forced into exile. His treatise on sales has the first discussion of *Raffles*. He summarized the principle in this fashion:

> If *A* and *B* contract for the sale of the cargo per ship Peerless, and there be two ships of that name, and *A* mean one ship and *B* intend the other ship, there is no contract. But if there be but one ship Peerless, and *A* sell the cargo of that ship to *B,* the latter would not be permitted to excuse himself on the ground that he had in his mind the ship Peeress, and intended to

contract for a cargo by this last-named ship. Men can only bargain by mutual communication, and if *A*'s proposal were unmistakable, as if it were made in writing, and *B*'s answer an unequivocal and unconditional acceptance, *B* would be bound, however clearly he might afterwards make it appear that he was thinking of a different vessel. For the rule of law is general, that whatever a man's real intention may be, if he manifests an intention to another party, so as to induce that other party to act upon it, he will be estopped from denying that the intention as manifested was his real intention.[9]

Everyone from Judah P. Benjamin to Holmes to Learned Hand can agree with the idea that parties to contracts adopt the formalities inherently associated with language. "Men can only bargain by mutual communication." If there is one ship *Peerless* and the contract unambiguously calls for cotton on the ship "Peerless," you cannot get off the hook by proving that you had the ship "Peeress" in mind when you entered into the deal. Everyone is both an objectivist and a formalist to at least this extent.

From the perspective of the practicing lawyer, the difference between a subjective and objective approach to the creation of the legally enforceable obligation may not, in fact, prove large. Even if a subjective test applied, parties must still introduce evidence that persuades a jury of their subjective intent. Twenty bishops are likely to be available to testify as to my subjective intentions only when these intentions were objectively manifest. Similarly, if an objective test controlled, my subjective intent provides indirect evidence. Ordinarily, someone who subjectively intends to sell salt will appear objectively to want to sell salt. My subjective intention to sell salt (evidenced perhaps by telling my friends about the deal) is probative of my objective conduct (what I actually told you).

Gravitating toward an objective test, however, has consequences. Once one adopts an objective test, one is no longer bound to look only for objective manifestations of intent. The objective test need not be a device aimed strictly at divining the party's thoughts or what most in that position would have intended. We might, for example, have legal rules designed to minimize miscommunication in the first place. For example, if I communicate with you by telegraph, and the telegraph company mistranscribes the price term and says that I am willing to sell for $9, when in fact I am willing to sell for only $10, a legal rule might hold me to selling for $9 if I am the person best positioned to ensure that the telegraph company transcribed my offer correctly. I would be bound to a bargain that I never intended. There might be plenty of objective evidence of my subjective intentions, but it would make no difference. Once we are unmoored from the idea that there needs to be a subjective meeting of the minds, we are no longer committed to finding a bargain in fact.

Holmes asserts that the objective test with respect to proper names is that people are entitled to rely on the association known to them, at least when their use of this association is not deceptive. But it is not the only test we might use. Rather than give individuals the privilege of insisting on the proper names known to them, we might hold merchants to the proper name that someone knowledgeable in the relevant trade would think they were using.

Liverpool merchants might, for example, have a norm that if someone used the word "Peerless" to refer to a ship en route from Bombay, that person was referring to the ship *Peerless* that had been reported in the Liverpool press as sailing from Bombay. Merchants were expected to use press reports as their starting point in communicating with other merchants. (Under this rule, a contract would exist and Wichelhaus would prevail, regardless of what Raffles subjectively thought.[10]) Or the rule might provide that others were entitled to assume that it was the ship *Peerless* that had sailed from India to Liverpool before. (Under this rule, Wichelhaus would again prevail.[11]) These sorts of tests go further than the objective tests like those of Benjamin, centered as they are on concrete evidence of subjective intent. We are no longer merely looking for evidence of intent (such as what the person actually said). We are instead requiring those who contract to express themselves in a particular way. A single lexicon is used to interpret what they are saying.

Henry Friendly, one of the great commercial law judges of the last century, confronted a modern analogue to *Raffles* in *Frigaliment Importing Co.* Buyer and seller both agreed that a deal had been formed but disagreed as to what the deal was. The case turned on the word "chicken":

> Plaintiff says "chicken" means a young chicken, suitable for broiling and frying. Defendant says "chicken" means any bird of that genus that meets contract specifications on weight and quality, including what it calls "stewing chicken" and plaintiff pejoratively terms "fowl." Dictionaries give both meanings, as well as some others not relevant here.[12]

Each of the parties put forward different objective tests, but each also agreed that "chicken" in the contract had a single objective meaning that bound both parties. The dispute was resolved in the end because the plaintiff bore the burden of proof, and he was unable to show that his favored lexicon should be used rather than the one the defendant proposed.

When an objective benchmark is used to assess meaning, cases like *Raffles* tend to appear only in the rare situations when each party is entitled to use her own lexicon. Ambiguity in a contract usually does not arise because of a failure of a proper name. And when describing goods and services, we are less likely to privilege any given individual's own usage. Parties are usually held to speak the same language. When disputes arise, parties are typically arguing not about whether an agreement came into being but rather about the meaning of the agreement.

One of the rare cases in which a court found that there was no bargain involved a misunderstanding on a construction project. Flower City agreed to do the painting in a new apartment building for which Gumina was the general contractor.[13] In its contract, Flower City promised to do painting in accordance with the painting specifications and plans of the project at the following rate: one-bedroom units at $335; two-bedroom units at $371; three- at $428; four- at $477. These numbers added up to $100,000.

Flower City thought it was going to paint only the interior of each apartment. Before the painting began, Flower City discovered that the builder believed it had promised to paint, in addition, the hallways, common rooms, and exterior doors. The two parties subjectively understood their deal differently. The builder insisted that Flower City paint the hallways and Flower City refused. The builder canceled the contract, and then Flower sued. The court concluded that each party was entitled to its own understanding of the contract.

One might think the outcome sensible. There is strong objective evidence that the parties gave different meanings to the same words. As we have seen, however, objective tests need not try to approximate what the parties might have been thinking. We might want a rule that induces the party with information to disclose it. When a contract has two possible meanings and one party is aware of the ambiguity and the other is not, the rule might provide that it is the party who knows of the ambiguity that must resolve the ambiguity or be held to the single meaning ascribed to the contract by the other side. If the general contractor knew both that the contract was ambiguous and that Flower City was under a misimpression, it had a duty to speak up.

The purpose of such a rule is not to try to capture a meeting of minds but rather to induce parties to be forthcoming when they bargain with one another. One court has called this "the duty of the forthright negotiator" and applied it between two highly sophisticated parties in a deal involving hundreds of millions of dollars.[14]

There are other ways to fashion objective tests. The misunderstanding in *Flower City* may have arisen because the painter was a newcomer and, as a newcomer, thought that "apartment" meant only interiors. We might give the general contractor an incentive to ensure that newcomers are not misled. The lexicon that applied between merchants in the same merchant community might not apply to newcomers who are unfamiliar with it.

None of these objective rules is necessarily a good idea. For example, rules designed to protect outsiders may make established merchants even more reluctant to deal with them. Inexperienced contractors like Flower City may never have their bids accepted in the first place. The rule may make entry harder, not easier.

For this reason, our objective rule might be that everyone is bound with the language in the contract as experienced people in a particular community understand it. We might hold a newcomer to the language of the trade, even if, measured objectively, we were confident that the newcomer did not know it. If you want to operate in a market, you must first learn its language.

These objective rules go further than the kind of objective rule that Benjamin advocated. We are not simply saying that you are stuck when you say "Peerless" and you mean "Peeress." We are insisting that you are held to paint the exterior hallways when you say "apartment" even when we know that people in your position mean something different when they use this word.

There is an element of formality here. We are binding Flower to a deal it never intended to enter. There was no meeting of the minds in any magical nineteenth-century sense. But it might be that a clear rule, such as this one, will work most of the time and make people better off. Indeed, at the margin, it should keep mistakes like this from happening in the future. To the extent that people know the legal rule, they will know that when they communicate, they have to use the language of the trade.

We should be cautious, however, about thinking that courts can readily identify a common language of the trade. Trade usage may not be clear. It may not be constant across time and place. And even if it were both clear and constant, a court may not be able to access it.[15] As we saw, Grant Gilmore himself misunderstood trade usage in trying to understand the role that the name of the ship played in contracts to arrive.

There is a deeper problem. It is often a mistake to infer legal obligations from the customs and practices of merchants. I once hired a contractor to remodel my apartment. I chose a high-end contractor. As such, he had a reputation for doing the job right and going the extra mile. At the end of the job, I needed some pictures hung. These were not part of the contract. I asked him to help me hang them. It was the end of a very long day, but he took a lot of pride in finishing a job right. He was willing to stay late and do things that were not in the contract. That is what high-end contractors do. That is why I hired him. But does my contractor have a legal obligation to hang pictures at the end of a long job? Is he bound to hang your pictures, even though you are not a nice person and have been nothing but trouble? Does the general practice that he and other upscale contractors follow with most of their clients generate a set of legal obligations that upscale contractors owe to everyone? Does the common practice among hotels of checking in guests early when rooms are available give rise to a legal obligation to check guests in early?

There is another problem. We are trying to extract legal rules from the norms that exist within a merchant community. But these norms arise from regular transactions within a single culture when things are going well. Lawsuits arise only when things have fallen apart. The norms from ordinary times may not be apt. Even if they were, lawsuits frequently involve amateurs or outsiders or people from different commercial cultures. In my culture an apartment means one thing; in your culture it means another. We cannot rely on usage of trade unless we know which usage we are supposed to choose.

Commercial practice arises in a particular context that is often hard for outsiders to divine. A historian in the distant future who knew nothing about the 1960s except a series of amendments to the rules of a country club would see the introduction of all sorts of rules requiring members to wear ties and jackets. She might infer that people's dress became increasingly formal and fastidious during this period. This historian, however, would be making a mistake because she did not understand the context. Such rules were not required at the club until the late 1960s because before then everyone wore a tie and jacket as a matter of course. Rules became necessary only because dress was becoming increasingly casual. Context always matters, and the relevant commercial practice is something we have to construct from fragmentary bits of evidence. The picture we piece together may give us less guidance than we think.

In addition, we have to form legal rules with some awareness of how parties naturally behave. Formal legal rules work best when everyone knows about them. Putting forward an objective rule and holding parties to it makes sense if it reinforces what people do anyway or if people know about the legal rule. As lawyers we have to be careful that we do not overstate the effect that the law has on conduct. We may have a legal formality that people do not know about. Or people may know about it, but it is so cumbersome that it is not worth bothering with in all cases just to get the desired result in the one stray case that gets litigated. Under such circumstances, objective rules that try to shape the conduct of the parties are worse than having no rule at all.

A formal rule helps parties to know where they stand only if they are aware of it. This is the *Dr. Strangelove* principle. In this Cold War dark comedy, the Russians invent a device that will destroy the world if the United States drops a nuclear weapon on them. The idea is that this "Doomsday machine" will provide an effective deterrent. The Russians, however, decide to keep the machine's existence a secret for a time. This, of course, defeats its purpose. A legal formality is like the Doomsday machine. Neither does any good unless people know about them.

Some element of formality, however, is inevitable. We need to have a clear understanding of when a contract comes into being. A mystical subjective meeting of the minds is too ethereal. We want people to know exactly when they are obliged and when they are not. Hence, we have an objective theory of contracts. Formation of a contract requires communication. When I make a promise in exchange for your promise, we each must try to understand the other.

To be sure, the usual predicate for contractual liability is an agreement between two parties. Asking whether there was an agreement in fact and what its terms were is nearly always a good place to start. But we should not become hung up on the idea that formation of a contract requires an act of the will merely because the basis of contract is consent.

Holmes solved the problem in *Raffles* by asserting that a particular convention existed with respect to proper names. People are entitled to assume that the proper name they use is the one that will form the basis of the contract. If people use a proper name differently and it is material, no contract is formed. Although not silly in principle, his take on the case has an ipse dixit quality to it. In the end, Holmes's success on this frontier lies not so much in offering a clever and counterintuitive reading of cases such as *Raffles* but rather in putting forward a sensible ground rule.

You are bound by what a reasonable third party would understand you to mean, even if you subjectively intended something else. You are much better able to make sure that you are being clear about your intentions than I am able to determine whether your inner thoughts in fact correspond to what you are saying. We are better off living in a world in which we can assess each other's objective actions according to benchmarks that are easily visible.

2

The Bargained-for Exchange

We are morally and ethically obliged to keep our promises, but it does not follow that promises should be legally enforceable on that account alone. Legal enforceability raises the stakes considerably. Holding a promise legally enforceable empowers one private citizen to call on the state to use force (if necessary) against another. It is not something to be done lightly, especially when the judge must try to reconstruct the promise in question from evidence that can be conflicting and incomplete.

We share intuitions about the cases at the extremes. The written promise of a giant corporation to sell goods to another giant corporation should be legally enforceable. A casual promise one friend makes to another in a social setting—perhaps about meeting for lunch or dinner—should not be. It would be surprising if any contemporary legal regime provided otherwise. But those trained in the law must learn about the cases that fall between these two extremes.

Hamer v. Sidway is one of these intermediate cases.[1] An uncle promises to give his fifteen-year-old nephew $5,000 on his nephew's twenty-first birthday if the young man promises in return not to smoke, drink, or play cards or billiards for money until then. The legal question the case presents is straightforward: If the nephew keeps his end of the bargain, is the uncle legally obliged to pay? Can the nephew, in other words, sue the uncle if he breaks his promise? This question has been a central preoccupation of contracts professors for over a hundred years. It has become the standard vehicle used to distinguish those promises that are legally enforceable from those that are not.

The uncle's promise was not made in the marketplace. We cannot easily point to something such as the desirability of mutually beneficial trade to justify legal enforceability. Conversely, the promise was not a casual one. The whole point of the uncle's promise was for the nephew to take it seriously. Therefore, we should not necessarily treat the uncle's promise as we would an ordinary social promise.

Successive generations of legal scholars looked at the bare facts of *Hamer v. Sidway* in quite different ways. In the first half of this chapter, I show how this case shaped the debate over the doctrine of consideration and promissory estoppel, a debate that occupied the attention of contracts scholars for decades. In the second half, I look at the case more closely to show how both accounts, in an effort to isolate a general principle, may have lost sight of what matters most.

Understanding *Hamer v. Sidway* and the challenges it presents requires locating the uncle and his nephew in a large family group portrait. In addition to his nephew, the uncle cared about his nieces and making sure that they were provided for. He also had to sort out his relationship with his older brother, someone who was financially dependent on him for much of his adult life. The extended family, like many others before and since, was one in which the more well-to-do looked out for those who were less fortunate. Outside of the commercial mainstream, social relationships are inevitably intricate and laden with ambiguity.

Before the nineteenth century, courts regularly insisted that only promises supported by "consideration" were legally enforceable. But defining exactly what constituted consideration proved elusive. Sometimes it seemed that "consideration" was simply the word courts attached to promises that they were willing to enforce. Holmes believed that consideration could be defined precisely.

By Holmes's account, consideration exists (and a promise is legally enforceable) if, but only if, there is a bargained-for exchange. Common law courts enforced only those promises that are made in return for something else. A mere promise is not enforceable. (I promise to pay you ten dollars.) A promise that is subject to a condition is not enforceable. (I promise to pay you ten dollars if you are around when I get my next paycheck.) A promise that is given in exchange for a benefit you confer on me (or a detriment you incur on yourself) is enforceable. (I promise to pay you ten dollars if in return you promise to mow my lawn.) The key to consideration is that the promise is given in return for the benefit or detriment.

The value of what was given in return for the promise does not matter, only that it was part of an exchange. In the words of Lord Coke, "a horse, a hawk, a robe would do."[2] There just has to be an exchange. A legally enforceable promise could not exist in the absence of a bargain. As Holmes put it,

> [I]t is the essence of a consideration that, by the terms of the agreement, it is given and accepted as the motive or inducement of the promise. Conversely, the promise must be made and accepted as the conventional motive or inducement for furnishing the consideration. The root of the whole matter is the relation of reciprocal conventional inducement, each for the other, between consideration and promise.[3]

Legal enforceability turns on whether there was consideration, and this, in turn, requires a bargained-for exchange. Holmes's understanding had become the conventional wisdom at least at the Harvard Law School when word of *Hamer v. Sidway* reached there in the fall of 1890.

The intermediate appellate court had handed down its opinion during the summer and held that the nephew's promise to refrain from smoking, drinking, and gambling was not sufficient consideration to make a promise legally enforceable.[4] The promise had no pecuniary value to the uncle and, far from being a detriment to the nephew, probably did him considerable good. For those steeped in the teaching of Holmes, however, this misunderstood the nature of consideration in a fundamental way.

If I commission an artist to paint a picture for a fixed sum, my obligation to pay the money is enforceable, regardless of whether I derive any value from the picture or whether the artist would have been happy to paint the picture without being paid. The fact of the bargain itself is all that matters. Further inquiry can be only a source of mischief. Returning to the facts of *Hamer*, to constitute consideration, it is enough that the nephew and the uncle each give up a legal right in exchange for a promise. How much performance works to the benefit of one or the detriment of the other is irrelevant, just as long as the performance (refraining from drinking, smoking, and gambling) is done in exchange for the promise of $5,000.

In short, from the perspective of anyone who adhered to Holmes's view of consideration, the intermediate court in *Hamer v. Sidway* had to be wrong. While the case was on appeal to New York's highest court, the *Harvard Law Review* criticized the intermediate court opinion on just these grounds:

> [T]o say that no legal detriment is involved . . . i.e., that no legal right is parted with, would probably surprise a good many persons. . . . [T]he

court's . . . suggestion, that even if there were an intention to contract the acts of the nephew, though performed at the uncle's request and in exchange for his promise, would not be a sufficient consideration, is surprising.[5]

The case finally reached New York's highest court, and it reversed the decision. We do not know whether any on the court read the *Harvard Law Review,* but it embraced the same view of consideration that permeated the halls of Harvard. It was enough that the nephew had a legal right to smoke, drink, and gamble and had agreed to give it up in exchange for the uncle's promise:

> We need not speculate on the effort which may have been required to give up the use of those stimulants. It is sufficient that he restricted his lawful freedom of action within certain prescribed limits upon the faith of his uncle's agreement, and now having fully performed the conditions imposed, it is of no moment whether such performance actually proved a benefit to the promisor.[6]

The record provided enough evidence to justify treating the uncle's promise as a bargained-for exchange. Willie's adolescence had gotten off to a rocky start. By the time he was fifteen, Willie had, by his own account, "indulged in a moderate degree of playing billiards, and smoking, and drinking beer and liquor."[7] The uncle viewed these developments with some alarm, observing, "You know when a boy of his age gets to going bad it always gains on him, and I want to hold out some inducement to stop it right here and now."[8]

The uncle called Willie over during a family celebration and couched what he told him in the language of a bargain. "Willie, I am going to make you a proposition. . . . If you will not drink any liquor, will not smoke, will not play cards or billiards until you are twenty-one, I will give you $5,000 that day." Willie understood his uncle to be proposing a bargain, and he took it as such. After some negotiating to ensure he could still play cards and billiards as long it was not for money, Willie accepted the uncle's "proposition." Willie, by his account at least, took the promise seriously. While he was away at college and fell quite ill, the doctor prescribed a medicine with alcohol in it, but he refused to take it.

On his twenty-first birthday, Willie again used the language of a bargained-for exchange when he wrote his uncle: "I believe, according to agreement, that there is due me $5,000. I have lived up to the contract to the letter in every sense of the word." The uncle, for his part, responded in similar terms, "Your letter . . . came to me saying that you had lived up to the promise made to me several years ago. I have no doubt but you have, for which you shall have five thousand dollars as I promised you."

The intermediate court focused narrowly on the question of consideration and found it wanting. This was sufficient to find against Willie. Hence, the question of whether the promise was supported by consideration became the focal point of his appeal. Instead of reviewing any of the many other issues raised in the record, the court simply took sides in a doctrinal dispute—and went with the side that was then the prevailing academic fashion.

Three years later, the same court found that a father's promise to give money to his daughter was unenforceable precisely because there was no quid pro quo.[9] It did not matter that the father went so far as to open an account in his daughter's name and put the money in it (something that the uncle in *Hamer v. Sidway* promised to do but never did). A promise is not enforceable in the absence of a bargained-for exchange, and the daughter had done nothing in return for the promise. Until the money (or the passbook controlling the account) was delivered, the law would do nothing to aid her.

Hamer as it was first told in the academy reflected Holmesian orthodoxy. A bargain must exist for a promise to be legally enforceable. Inside the family, explicit bargains are the exception. Hence, most intrafamilial promises are, in this world, not legally enforceable. *Hamer* is an exception that proves the rule.

Hamer v. Sidway entered the canon to illustrate the idea that a bargained-for promise was enforceable, regardless of what was being promised and regardless of the social environment in which it took place. It was enough that the bargained-for consideration involved giving up a legal right. That the facts were extreme and unusual did not matter at all. Indeed, it underscored the idea that a principle was at work that lived apart from the particular facts of a case. It emphasized that any bargain, even over such a matter as teenage smoking and drinking, was enforceable, as long as there was, in fact, a bargain.

For Holmes, the task of the legal scholar was simply one of being a careful observer. Like the Young Astronomer who coldly and dispassionately charts the heavens, Holmes provided a descriptive account of what the courts did. Samuel Williston, the person who succeeded Langdell at Harvard as its foremost authority on contracts, followed a similar path. He was even less interested in explaining why enforcing the promise in a case such as *Hamer v. Sidway* was a sound way to organize human affairs.

The generation that followed Williston, however, thought such a justification necessary. Principal among them was Arthur Corbin, Yale's foremost exponent on contract. He questioned the idea that the artificial notion of a bargained-for exchange standing alone could sensibly draw a line between those promises that should be legally enforceable and those that should not be. *Hamer v. Sidway* was one of many cases in which courts enforced promises that fit only awkwardly with blackletter law.

Someone coming to *Hamer v. Sidway* from this perspective could take the facts as recounted at trial and tell a different story. At the family celebration, the uncle was merely adding a condition to a promise made long before. Willie was named after his uncle, and his uncle had always been fond of him. Even when Willie was as young as eight or ten, the uncle frequently told Willie's father and mother that he had $5,000 on deposit in the bank earmarked for Willie. Willie would have it when he turned twenty-one.[10]

This testimony comes from a former family retainer who lived in the Midwest and had to testify through interrogatories, far away from the family lawyers. Although she appears anxious to do everything she can to support her former employers, the inability of the lawyers to coach her may have led to an account that focuses more on the seriousness with which the uncle made the promise, rather than on his making it as part of a bargained-for exchange.

Rather than a deal made to get Willie's life in order, the insistence that Willie cut out his bad habits was simply a string the uncle tied to a promise. There was never a bargain. The uncle believed that "when Willie came of age, if everything was favorable, he would start him in business and help him, and . . . this $5,000 would be something to look forward to that would stimulate him to do right, and if he was steady and industrious this would be a good start; and if he was not, this would be enough for him to squander."[11]

Someone looking at the case from this perspective would see that making legal liability turn on the existence of a bargained-for exchange was pernicious. It forced lawyers to reshape Willie and his father's account of the uncle's promise into the procrustean bed of a bargained-for exchange or, failing that, find another route to legal enforceability. Far from being an example of a narrow conception of what promises were legally enforceable, this case belonged to a large class of cases where courts had found in favor of promisees even though the promises were outside the marketplace. A relative asks another to come live with them and let them build a house, promising to convey the land beneath.[12] A grandfather promises money to his granddaughter so that she would leave her job.[13] In dozens of cases, using a number of different theories, courts enforced promises that were seriously made as long as they were reasonably relied on.[14]

Parties might be able to argue that there was a bargained-for exchange, but it made no sense to require them to do so. The uncle made a promise, knowing that his nephew would rely on it. In this and in many other cases, courts found such promises legally enforceable, independent of whether the promise was part of a bargained-for exchange. To describe accurately what courts did, the narrow doctrine of a consideration in the form of a bargained-for exchange was not enough.[15]

Corbin wanted to focus on the world as it was and draw conclusions about the structure of the law from "prevailing notions of honor and well-being, notions that grow out of ages of experience in business affairs and in social intercourse."[16] Corbin was a revolutionary only in a limited sense. He did not advocate dramatic change, and he still thought that the legal principles of a society were things that could be discovered. Legal principles, however, were not immutable truths but rather principles that could be derived from norms that command broad acceptance.

We can understand Corbin's approach to the question of what promises should be legally enforceable by returning to *Hamer v. Sidway*. A court might easily find that there was a promise subject to a condition, rather than a bargained-for exchange. For Williston, which story one told was all important. For Corbin, it did not make any difference. In Corbin's view, the seriousness of the promise and Willie's reliance on it was decisive. If the promise in *Hamer* was enforceable, then so too should be an uncle's wholly gratuitous promise if a nephew went to college in reliance on it. What matters is that the behavior reasonably and predictably changed as a result of the promise, not that this behavior was tied explicitly to the promise.

For Corbin, the idea that reasonable reliance on a promise should trigger legal liability could be derived from existing mores. The norm that a decent person keeps any serious promise that another relies on is strongly held. Therefore, the reliance itself provides a ground for making the promise legally enforceable.

There is much to admire in Corbin's work. We must credit Corbin with the insight that consideration is itself a convention that falls far short of being an independent and immutable law that definitively establishes the domain of legally enforceable promises. Corbin's introduction of reliance as an organizing principle gave decisive shape to the way contracts was taught for most of the twentieth century. The principle of promissory estoppel—that someone in the uncle's position is legally obliged to keep serious promises that were reasonably relied on, at least to the extent of the reliance—remains part of the modern law of contract.

In practice, however, the idea of promissory estoppel has proved far more modest than one would guess from the way it is presented in first-year contracts classes.[17] There are relatively few litigated cases in which a promise is made with sufficient definiteness that it justifies reasonable reliance and yet still lacks sufficient consideration to support enforcement along conventional lines. The reporters are filled with opinions that set out the elements of promissory estoppel, affirm its continuing vitality, and then find that it does not apply to the facts before the court.

Moreover, Corbin and his heirs fell short in constructing a compelling theory of promissory estoppel. The principle that promises relied on should be enforced demands justification. By their own account, it was contingent on fact and circumstance, not an immutable law of nature. Too many who followed in Corbin's footsteps thought the virtues of such a rule required no explanation, but these virtues are far from self-evident. Once one grounds the question of legal enforceability on what makes for sound practice, one should explain why making such promises legally enforceable is a good idea. Given the extralegal pressures that are at work, the limited competence of courts, and the costs that come with making a promise legally enforceable, we cannot say that enforcing promises reasonably relied on follows ineluctably from the notion that keeping promises is a good thing. Nor can we say that it solves the hard cases.

Recall the facts of *Allegheny College*.[18] A widow promised to leave a bequest to a college and then changed her plans. The college sued to enforce the promise against her estate. Benjamin Cardozo found that there was consideration and hence the promise was enforceable. As he showed time and time again, Cardozo could find consideration anywhere:

The promisor wished to have a memorial to perpetuate her name. . . . [T]here was an assumption of a duty [on the part of the college] to do whatever acts were customary or reasonably necessary to maintain the memorial fairly and justly. . . .

Cardozo goes on at length to explain how this gift was part of a bargained-for exchange. Corbin wished that judges did not have to make such heroic stretches of the doctrine of consideration. He thought judges should be able to look at the reality of these situations. The presence of reliance would tell us that this promise was one we should enforce.

Corbin is right to point to the ways that courts had to bend the idea of a bargained-for exchange. Indeed, the very malleability of the doctrine makes it suspect as a formal rule. A doctrine so capable of being recast may not do much to let parties know where they stand. But does the idea of reliance do the slightest bit of good here? How exactly did the college rely in this case? Was it reasonable? Moreover, Corbin thought that these promises to charities should be enforceable as a general matter. How do we get this out of the idea of reliance? The *Restatement (Second) of Contracts* virtually concedes this point by declaring that in the case of charitable subscriptions, reliance is presumed.

Those cases in which promissory estoppel matters outside the marketplace are often cases where something happened offstage that the judge cannot see. The facts are likely to be hard to penetrate, and the way the judge constructs the story is especially likely to be wrong. Perhaps as important, the intricate social relationships outside the marketplace rarely reduce themselves easily to a framework in which the rights of A and B can be rigorously defined.

Once we leave the world of commerce, genuine misunderstandings can easily arise. *Mills v. Wyman,*[19] one of the other canonical cases used to illustrate the deficiencies in the traditional doctrine of consideration, presents precisely this sort of difficulty. By the usual account of this case, a stranger takes into his house a young man who has fallen ill. The Good Samaritan writes to the young man's father, and the father writes back promising to pay his expenses. Subsequently, the father reneges on his promise and is sued. The court finds that the father's promise is not supported by consideration. The judge chastises the father for failing to honor his moral obligation but again, by the standard account, rigidly and mechanically insists that the promise is not legally enforceable.

This result is commonly criticized as an exemplar of equity being sacrificed in the name of rigid formalism. But before reaching this conclusion, we should first recognize that we confront exceedingly odd facts. The stranger had no obligation to the son but took him in and acted as a Good Samaritan. The father had no obligation to reimburse the Good Samaritan but promised to do so nevertheless. At this point, two unusual things happen. The father unaccountably breaks a promise he never had to make, and then the Good Samaritan seeks money for his good deed. Grateful parents usually do not renege; Good Samaritans are not supposed to be in it for the cash.

Something is going on, and the question in the first instance is whether a court can enter such shoals and, by enforcing the promise, make matters better. Refusing to enforce a promise in this environment may be less a mechanical adherence to the letter of the law than a recognition that the judge may not know enough to decide such cases wisely. Too much else is likely going on. A good judge, like a good doctor, should always remember Hippocrates: *First, do no harm.*

What we know about the facts of *Mills v. Wyman* allows a narrative rather different from the one we see in first-year casebooks.[20] Unstated in the opinion is the crucial fact that Mills, the Good Samaritan, was by profession an innkeeper.[21] He may have kept an inn, or he might have been someone who took on regular boarders. He might have had a common law obligation to take the son in. In any event, he took in young Wyman in the expectation that he would be paid. We also know that young Wyman had long been estranged from his father and had regularly incurred debts that his father refused to honor.

The trouble starts when young Wyman falls ill. Mills realizes that he has a lodger who is going to require a lot of care and who can no longer foot the bill. Mills is not a bad person, and he does not want to throw this lodger out onto the street, but he is, after all, in business, and he cannot make money by taking care of total strangers who do not pay their way. Young Wyman suggests that his father can pay the bill, and so Mills writes to him and the father writes back. The letter reads, in full:[22]

Dear Sir

I received a line from you relating to my Son Levi's sickness and requesting me to come up and see him, but as the going is very bad I cannot come up at the present, but I wish you to take all possible care of him and if you cannot have him at your house I wish you to remove him to some convenient place and if he cannot satisfy you for it I will.

I want that you should write me again immediately how he does and greatly oblige your most obedient servant

Seth Wyman
Shrewsbury Feb 24th 1821
Mr. Daniel Mills

The ambiguities in this letter suggest the following story. This case is one of a misunderstanding between two individuals, each of whom acted in good faith. The father mistakenly thinks Mills is a gentleman and a Good Samaritan, not an innkeeper. He never thought that Mills would charge for taking care of his son. He does, however, realize that Mills could not be expected to put him up forever. Wyman, therefore, tells Mills that if his son cannot stay at his house (for nothing, because house guests at the home of a gentleman do not pay), Mills should put him up at an inn. If the son cannot pay for this (as yet unincurred) expense, the father will. The father does not say he will pay Mills for keeping his son in his own home, either for the past or the future. Gentlemen do not charge each other for such things, but as a gentleman, the father feels obliged to cover another gentleman's out-of-pocket costs arising from the care of his son, even if he is estranged from his son and does not cover his debts with tradesmen.

Mills reads the letter differently. He thinks Wyman knows he is an innkeeper. He understands the letter to say that Wyman wants him to continue to board the son or find him some other boarding house, and Wyman will make good the expenses. From an innkeeper's perspective, the natural interpretation of the letter is not that the father will pay only for future expenses but that he will be good for everything. After all, the father wants him to do many things (such as find his son another place to stay if it proves necessary and secure medical care) that innkeepers usually do not do. Seen in this light, the father by this letter is promising to take care of the entire bill, if Mills continues to take care of Wyman's son or finds someone else who will. In other words, the father thinks he wrote the following letter:

Dear [Fellow Gentleman]:
   I wish you to take all possible care of him and if you cannot have him at your [home], I wish you to remove him to some convenient place and if he cannot satisfy you for [the cost of staying at such a place], I will.

Mills thinks he received this one:

Dear [Innkeeper]:
   I wish you to take all possible care of him. [ ] If you cannot have him at your [inn], I wish you to remove him to some convenient place[.] If he cannot [make you whole for everything], I will.

This retelling of the story explains why the case was litigated. Seth Wyman had no intention of paying off another one of his wayward son's bad debts. He promised a fellow gentleman to reimburse future out-of-pocket costs. He never promised an innkeeper to pay for obligations his son had already incurred, any more than he promised to pay any other creditors of his son. By contrast, Mills thought he had a perfectly conventional bargained-for exchange. The father asked him, someone in the business of lodging people, to take all possible care of the son, and if the son could not pay the bill, the father would. If Mills continued to take care, the father would pay for everything. Mills's undertaking to continue to provide care was consideration for the father's promise to pick up the entire bill. The misunderstanding—and the cultural divide between a gentleman and a tradesman—gave rise to the litigation.

This account of *Mills v. Wyman* may be no more accurate than the conventional one, but behind any set of facts are many possible narratives. Holmes and his successors thought all that was necessary was to ask whether the facts could be recast as a narrative involving a bargained-for exchange; Corbin and the generations that followed believed that one could apply principles that ensure that promises seriously made were enforced to the extent that justice required. Neither recognized how much context matters. The bargained-for exchange is an imperfect formal rule because it is so malleable. Reliance is an imperfect standard because it slights the difficulties inherent in making promises enforceable, even when seriously made and taken seriously.

The record such as the one we find in *Hamer v. Sidway* allows for multiple narratives as well. We can tell different stories, depending on the point of view we take and the facts we use. One underscores the challenges of making promises outside the commercial mainstream legally enforceable; another shows the limited work that the law can perform in an environment in which relationships are often (and sometimes necessarily) incompletely developed.

Observe the story of *Hamer v. Sidway* from the point of view of Franklin Sidway. Franklin Sidway is William's executor. Sidway is vice president of the Farmers and Mechanics National Bank, a man who is "prudent, conservative, quick of decision, and not afraid of large undertakings."[23] As a banker whose job it is to handle such matters, Sidway is used to the disputes that arise from probating the estates of wealthy individuals. Another prominent citizen of Buffalo was appointed to act as co-executor, but he declines, perhaps seeing that the matter would be a contentious one.

Sidway is the person in the first instance who must decide whether the estate is bound to honor the promise. Lawyers who have represented Willie and his family for years approach Franklin Sidway and ask him to make good on the promise William made to Willie long before. Formally, they are representing not Willie himself but rather Louise Hamer. She is Willie's mother-in-law, and, Sidway is told, she is entitled to enforce this odd promise because Willie assigned it to her shortly after his uncle's funeral. Sidway is used to dealing with lawyers over such matters. Far from having an animus against Willie's lawyers, Sidway was using them at the same time in another piece of litigation.[24]

Precisely because he is neither a family member nor a friend who cares about sorting out the equities after the fact, Sidway's focus is narrowly on the facts and the legal technicalities. He is skeptical. At the start, the evidence that the promise had even been made is not ironclad. There is only a copy, in Willie's hand, of the uncle's letter.[25] Even after Sidway is persuaded that the letter is genuine, Sidway doubts that Willie lived up to his part of the bargain. Willie freely admits that he smoked, drank, and gambled both before he was fifteen and again after he was twenty-one. He spent a good part of the intervening time at college in Ann Arbor, Michigan, hundreds of miles away from the eyes of anyone in his hometown. When asked about his college experiences, Willie has trouble remembering the names of his classmates or where they might be found. The only one Willie can remember and locate is, it appears, a relative of his lawyer.[26]

These problems are only the first of many reasons Sidway has for not recognizing the claim. Even if Willie had once been able to bring the action against his uncle, William seems to have satisfied whatever obligations he owed Willie by setting him up in business, not once but twice. Shortly after turning twenty-one, Willie and his father borrowed $5,000 from the uncle as part of their efforts to run a dry goods business.[27] This loan was never repaid. When William set up his brother and his son in business a second time, he insisted that they both sign "a good strong release." The release Willie signed

forever discharged the said William E. Story, his heirs, executors, and administrators, . . . from all . . . causes of action, . . . suits, debts, . . . sums of money . . . which against the said William E. Story [Willie] ever had, now ha[s], or which [Willie] . . . hereafter can, shall or may have, for or upon or by reason of any matter, cause or thing whatsoever, from the beginning of the world to the day of the date of these presents.[28]

Even if the uncle had not kept his promise to give $5,000 to Willie, and even if he had not obtained a release from him (either one of which extinguishes any claim Willie might have against the estate), Willie lost any right to bring the action for yet another reason. When the first business failed, Willie filed for bankruptcy. In that bankruptcy, any legally enforceable right he might have had against the uncle was necessarily turned over to his creditors. And, of course, the largest of these creditors was his uncle.

In short, Sidway is convinced that, quite apart from William having kept his promise (twice), the complaint is fatally defective for at least two additional reasons: (1) Willie gave up his right to enforce the promise when he turned over his assets (including any choses in action) to his creditors when he filed for bankruptcy; and (2) he lost whatever rights he had against the uncle when he later signed the release. Sidway moves to dismiss the complaint, believing it will disappear quickly.

The family's lawyers, however, file an amended complaint. They say they made a mistake in drafting the first one. After the uncle died, it was Willie's wife, and not Willie himself, who made the transfer to Louise Hamer.[29] Willie assigned his uncle's promise to his wife, it is now alleged, *before* he filed for bankruptcy or signed the release. Once transferred, neither his bankruptcy nor the release affected the enforceability of the promise. Willie's wife still held the promise at the time the uncle died, and her transfer of the promise to her mother, again shortly after the uncle's funeral, was therefore effective.

Sidway suspects that Willie came up with the story of the assignment to his wife only after reading the reply to the complaint. But even if he had made the assignment, it is still by no means obvious that the assignment was effective. By Willie's own account, he made the assignment gratuitously just a few weeks before his bankruptcy petition, and, again by his own account, he did it for the express purpose of keeping this asset beyond the reach of his creditors (the largest of whom was, of course, his uncle). Making a secret, gratuitous transfer to a close relative on the eve of bankruptcy is as flagrant a fraudulent conveyance as one might imagine. Failing to disclose it in the bankruptcy was a capital crime through the eighteenth century. In the nineteenth century, as in our own time, such transfers could be set aside and, if discovered, lead to a denial of discharge.[30] It is hard to imagine a principle more firmly embedded in the law. When Willie produces the release, he seems oblivious to fraudulent conveyance law and even claims that before he did it he consulted with his lawyers, the same ones involved in this litigation.[31]

Sidway does not buy any of this. Quite apart from whether Willie kept his end of the bargain while in Ann Arbor or whether the uncle kept his by setting Willie up in business, the fraudulent conveyance is a showstopper. If either Willie's wife or Louise herself had given value for the promise, she might be able to enforce it, but as neither had, Louise's rights against the uncle are no better than her son-in-law's.

Willie and his relatives now come back with a new factual claim to surmount this objection. This one, too, falls short of being completely convincing. Willie's father testifies that the uncle was later told about the fraudulent assignment after the bankruptcy and gave it his blessing. Even if we credit the father's story that the uncle blessed Willie's fraudulent assignment of the promise to his wife, it gives additional reason to think the promise was not intended to be (and was not understood by Willie to be) legally enforceable. The father reported that in the course of approving of the transfer, his brother added that he "should not let him nor her have the money until he thought they could take care of it."[32] In other words, at the same time he acquiesced in the assignment, William made it clear that he retained the exclusive power to decide when to make the payment.

By this point, Sidway has heard enough and refuses to settle. From Sidway's vantage point, each new explanation makes it clearer that the complaint is built on sand.[33] The story as a whole does not hold together. There are too many weak links. If the uncle were still alive, it is almost inconceivable that he could have been forced to pay. At every turn, the uncle made it clear that he would turn over the money only when he thought the time was right. The decision to turn over the money was one that, in the uncle's view, was exclusively his, not Willie's, not his mother-in-law's, and not a court's. At least one of the links—that the uncle blessed the fraud Willie perpetrated on him—rests on the flimsiest of evidence that any testimony from the uncle would have dispelled.

Franklin Sidway's frustration with the case may reflect a lack of comfort with a peculiarity of Anglo-American law. It breaks causes of action into discrete elements. Each link in the story that Willie and his relatives need to tell to make the promise enforceable is weak. Nevertheless, to win they need show only that each link is more likely than not. Each of the factual claims (that there was a bargained-for exchange, that Willie kept the promise, that the uncle did not discharge the promise either time he set Willie up in business, that Willie did make the assignment to his wife, that the uncle blessed it) leaves ground for doubt, but as long as the fact finder believes each of them standing alone to be just a little more likely than not, the promise is enforceable, even if in the aggregate the probability that all are true is small.[34]

In assessing the equities, it should be remembered that Willie's omission from the will was likely deliberate. To be sure, there was no falling out between the two and no event that would lead the uncle to renege on his promise.[35] But Willie grew up, married, and moved away. As their paths diverged, the uncle's affections and attentions went elsewhere, perhaps to the nieces living with him at the time he died.[36]

Nor is there any evidence that the uncle was casual in keeping his affairs and simply forgot about the $5,000. He maintained a separate account for one of his nieces, and he could have easily done so for his nephew. At least from the time that Willie turned twenty-one, the uncle had made it clear that Willie would have the $5,000 only when he, the uncle, thought the time right. That time never came to pass, most likely because the original purpose of the promise was to set up Willie in business, and the uncle had done this not once but twice. He likely thought that doing this (something that cost him considerably more than $5,000) was sufficient to discharge whatever obligation he owed.

The story behind *Hamer v. Sidway* should make Corbin's heirs uneasy. Enforcing all promises seriously made and reasonably relied on makes sense only if courts can engage in fact-finding with sufficient precision. Even without reaching any of the other complications in the story (of which there are many), the uncertainties around whether Willie even kept his side of the bargain alone provide a powerful counter to the intuition that promises seriously made and relied on should be legally enforceable. Such an approach leaves to a jury the question of whether the promise was kept and trusts the lawyer's skill at tracking down and then cross-examining Willie's college friends. Why would someone in the uncle's position want to risk such a thing when he makes a gratuitous promise? And why should we force it on him?

The further the promise from the marketplace, the more likely it has conditions implicit and explicit. Understanding what a promise means as circumstances change in a fluid social setting is a complicated business. Moreover, making a promise legally enforceable brings costs along with it. Litigation is expensive and prone to error. One should not blindly accept the syllogism that because keeping promises is good, making them legally enforceable is even better. It is one thing to say that I am morally bound to keep any promise I make seriously and quite another thing to say that when I make such a promise, I must expose myself to a swearing contest with my nephew's fraternity brothers.

If we look at the case again from the position of nineteenth-century formalists, we may find it less troubling. To be sure, at least since the time Willie turned twenty-one, the uncle insisted that he had complete discretion over whether to turn over the money. Willie knew this early on and did not object over the course of more than a decade. If either thought the promise was intended to be legally enforceable, he would have acted differently. But we can nevertheless reconcile the outcome with traditional doctrine in the same way one can reconcile anomalous outcomes under any formal legal rule. Formal rules by their nature are over- and underinclusive. The idea of a bargained-for exchange works well over the vast majority of cases. This case may be the odd one in which it does not work well. Moreover, if the uncle had not wanted his promise to be legally enforceable, he should not have couched it in terms of a bargain. People who use the language of a bargained-for exchange who do not intend their promises to be legally enforceable do so at their peril.

The idea of focusing on the bargained-for exchange usually makes sense, and if we simply direct the fact finder to determine whether William intended to make his promise legally enforceable, we are likely to go wrong. Indeed, by relying on the uncle's probable intent to guide us, we may become too smug and too comfortable with what we are doing. We shall purport to be answering the question, "What did the uncle intend?" but, in fact, we shall be continuing to ask whether we think that it is a good idea that this promise should be enforced, given all the facts and circumstances.

To find fault with Holmes or Corbin is not the same as coming up with a legal rule that is better. How exactly should one identify the domain of legally enforceable promises? If a general inquiry into intent is too slippery, if bargained-for consideration and reasonable reliance are unsatisfactory, what are the alternatives? Before answering this question, it is useful to examine the larger context in which the controversy in *Hamer v. Sidway* plays itself out.

Another reconstruction of *Hamer v. Sidway* focuses not on Franklin Sidway but on William and his relationship with James, his older brother (and Willie's father). William Story was a "man of generous impulses, and though rather brusque in manner, had really a kind heart."[37] A lifelong bachelor, he had been a successful businessman who, after earning his fortune, retired in his early fifties. James Story had a much different life than his brother. He married and raised a family, but far from enjoying his younger brother's success, James had been a failure. The two brothers, however, had always been on good terms. William visited his older brother frequently. A room in James's house was set aside for William, and Willie, of course, was named after his uncle.[38]

James turned to his younger brother for support many times over the years. William helped him start a business on at least two occasions. When William died after a short illness at the age of sixty-three, he left only a modest bequest to his brother and likely left the bulk of his estate to his nieces. Their father (the youngest of the three brothers) had died some years before, and two of the nieces were living with William at the time he died.

Shortly after William's funeral, James and Willie met with the family lawyers in Buffalo and arranged for them to assert whatever legal rights they might have against William Story's estate. To do this, the two assigned gratuitously all their rights against the estate to Louise Hamer, Willie's mother-in-law. Their reasons for calling so quickly on the family lawyers and making "arrangements for bringing suits and claims and all that sort of thing"[39] are lost to us. As in *Mills v. Wyman,* however, the record suggests one.

The relationship between William and James had always been partially business and partially familial. Money was always an issue. William was the largest creditor in his brother's bankruptcy. Indeed, he was the one who precipitated it. In James's words, "I went into bankruptcy at the suggestion of my brother. He said if I didn't go he would compel me to go."[40] Because he had taken the precaution of taking collateral for loans to his brother, William ended up with most of the property, while the other creditors received fifteen cents on the dollar.

Money also entered into the picture when it came to taking care of their own father a few years later. A widower, the father fell ill and became demented. William was unwilling to take care of him and persuaded his older brother to do it in return for $150 a month (over and above their father's expenses, which William would also cover). When asked to explain why he accepted $150 a month "for taking care of your own father in your own house from your own brother,"[41] James explained, "My father was crazy. I was poor, my brother was rich."[42]

This case may be one of the many we have in which the estate planning is incomplete. William likely consciously chose not to leave anything to his nephew Willie, believing he had already honored whatever commitment he had made. The treatment of his brother is another matter, however. At the time of his death, the relationship may have been one in which business and personal were merged. After James's business failed, we know that on more than one occasion his brother would buy a house, and James would live in it while renovating it.[43] This process of "fixing over" houses may have been a way for William to support his brother without putting his older brother in the position of taking an overt handout.

Because William died unexpectedly after only a short illness at the age of sixty-three, he may have not yet confronted the question of incorporating this ongoing, loose arrangement into his estate plan. If James still lived in a house that his brother owned and in which he wished to remain, he would have to buy it from the estate. In other words, William's unexpected death might have left James without a place to live.

James may have turned to his son for help, and Willie may have in turn gone to his mother-in-law. She might have agreed to help, but if she had, it would have made sense for them to assign whatever rights they had against the estate to her so they could be offset against whatever she had to pay for the house. This account explains why James, who was poor and who stood to inherit something from William, would make a gratuitous assignment of this bequest to his son's mother-in-law right after the funeral. The case itself may have concluded not with a payment from Franklin Sidway to Louise Hamer but rather with a credit against money she owed the estate as a result of the purchase of a house for her son-in-law's father.

In any event, Willie's side of the family consolidated whatever rights it had against the uncle's estate and put them in the hands of Louise Hamer.[44] There is no doubt that at the core of *Hamer v. Sidway* is a series of intrafamilial wealth transfers. The tension, in other words, is between William's young nieces and James, William's indigent seventy-year-old brother. In all of this, Willie is a bystander. Rather than the wayward adolescent being paid to hew to the straight and narrow, Willie is a responsible adult trying to find the means to care for his father. The complications that give rise to the litigation arise not from a gratuitous promise but from a long and complicated business and personal relationship between two brothers that comes to an end when one of them dies unexpectedly.

The larger story of *Hamer v. Sidway* is not about a single promise intended to curtail teenage smoking and drinking but rather about a number of complicated relationships inside an extended family. In this story, what role should the law play? How, for example, would things have played themselves out if, instead of bargained-for consideration, we had a formal rule that made a promise inside the family legally enforceable only if it were accompanied with a requisite level of formality, such as a notarized written document?

The standard objection to requiring legal rituals is that the parties will not know about them or be willing to spend the time and money they require. Willie and his family, however, provide evidence to the contrary. They were eager to take advantage of legal forms. Indeed, Willie's naive belief in legal formalities (an eve-of-bankruptcy transfer to his wife regular in form only) is one of the sources of difficulty.

Imagine that an intrafamily promise such as the one that William made Willie is legally enforceable and assignable only if it is notarized. If we focus narrowly on the facts of *Hamer v. Sidway* as usually recounted, such a rule exhibits distinct virtues. Willie and his uncle had a number of transactions over the years (including the execution of a release) that were heavily lawyered. The uncle would have been aware of a rule that required promises to be notarized to be enforceable. The uncle might have declined to go through the necessary ritual or he might have done so. The rule would have forced him to make his intentions clear. Given the amount of money involved and the explicit quid pro quo, there seems no harm in this.

But this is only one part of the story. Although a formal rule would have come to the aid of the Storys in the case of the promise between the uncle and the nephew, it cannot help with what may have been the principal problem the parties faced—unscrambling the relationship between the two brothers. Some relationships in a family are not spelled out and cannot be. James may have believed that his brother participated in his various ventures at arm's length. In his own mind, he was not taking any handouts from his younger brother. For his part, William may not have thought, and may not have wanted to think, about exactly how much he was in business with his brother and how much he was supporting him. There are virtues in open-ended relationships that leave much undeveloped.[45] But there are costs as well.

There are many cases, especially from this period, in which courts confront disappointed relatives who did not receive under a will what they had been promised.[46] Courts struggle to reconcile the law of trusts and estates, contract doctrine, and the dictates of equity. The larger story of *Hamer v. Sidway* underscores that in our legal system, as in every legal system, there are limits to what the law can do. In particular, our legal culture is one in which the law reduces relationships to discrete transactions and specified rights. There are many virtues to this legal culture, but such a legal system can do little when the problem is not a broken promise but rather a relationship that has never been formalized and perhaps could not have been. A discrete rights-based conception of law often maps poorly onto what happens inside a family and other social settings where, in our society at least, many relationships are incompletely reasoned.

It would be a mistake to think any legal rule we fashion will make perfect sense of the promise between William and Willie standing as it does in the shadow of far more complicated relationships between William and his brother, between William and his nieces, between Willie and his father, and between Willie and his mother-in-law. Finding that someone in Willie's position bargained with his uncle or reasonably relied on his promise as a teenager does remarkably little to unravel this web, one in which the law has only a supporting role.

3

Holmes's Bad Man

In the winter of 1897, Oliver Wendell Holmes, Jr., was fifty-five and languishing as an associate justice on a state supreme court.[1] He seemed destined to remain forever in the shadow of his father, the well-known man of letters who had died only a few years before. He was still determined to make sense of the law. Holmes was invited to give a talk at Boston University, and having little to lose, he chose to be provocative. He told this group of law students and young lawyers that "[i]f you want to know the law and nothing else, you must look at it as a bad man, who cares only for the material consequences which such knowledge enables him to predict, not as a good one, who finds his reasons for conduct, whether inside the law or outside of it, in the vaguer sanctions of conscience."[2]

What are we to make of this observation? Many have taken Holmes to task for this bloodless and detached view of life in general and the law in particular.[3] The novelist who portrayed Holmes as "The Young Astronomer" many years before conveys exactly this impression. He faulted Holmes for devoting all his time to observing the heavens and separating himself from all human interaction. It was wrong to spend all of one's time "looking at life as at a solemn show where he is only a spectator."[4] Of course, you are not cold, distant, and unfeeling merely because some writer paints you this way, but the writer in question was Oliver Wendell Holmes, Sr. When your own father tells the world you are distant and uncaring, you might wonder whether there is not something to it.

Remoteness and an absence of moral understanding do seem recipes for bad judging. Judges should not be distant spectators. When they are, they are wont to err and display a heartlessness incompatible with notions of fundamental justice.[5] Such individuals are all too likely to conclude, as

Holmes himself did in approving a law authorizing forced sterilization, that "three generations of imbeciles are enough."[6]

The link most believe exists between law and morals has led many to be equally critical of what comes next in "The Path of the Law"—the observation that "[t]he duty to keep a contract at common law means a prediction that you must pay damages if you do not keep it."[7] Here again, something important seems to be missing. Few think themselves free to break a promise and write a check instead. The existence of a legal obligation is a reason to perform that act, independent of the likelihood of a legal sanction. Most people think that when they make a promise, they should keep it, independent of the legal consequences attached to it. Breaking a promise and then paying damages is not the same as keeping a promise in the first place.

Holmes's "bad man" view of the common law and his effort to capture contractual liability as an option to perform or pay damages grew out of a debate he was having with another legal scholar in an exchange of letters that has largely been forgotten.[8] This chapter focuses on that scholar's critique of Holmes and the light it sheds on contract law generally.[9]

In 1895, Edward Avery Harriman was a young contracts professor teaching at Northwestern University. He had just published the opening chapter of his book on contracts, entitled "The Nature of Contractual Obligation."[10] Harriman sought "a scientific system of jurisprudence."[11] One needed to go beyond the technicalities of common law pleading. Tying contractual obligations to procedural forms did not itself provide a coherent account of the law. As Harriman put it, it was "about as satisfactory as a method of classification to the student of jurisprudence as the classification of flowers or rocks by their color would be to the botanist or geologist."[12] Simply cataloguing the forms of action available to victims of broken promises is not the same thing as having a theory. As Lord Kelvin reminded us, there are two kinds of science: physics and stamp collecting. In a world where too many were content with the latter, Harriman wanted to do the former.

Harriman, as many young law professors have done since, sent his paper to a senior scholar whom he especially admired—in his case Justice Holmes. In Holmes, he found a sympathetic ear. Harriman had, after all, enthusiastically adopted Holmes's objective theory of contract. As Holmes had already set out in *The Common Law* and was to reiterate in "The Path of the Law," the existence of a legally enforceable contract did not turn on whether there was any subjective meeting of the minds. What matters is what parties say, not what they intend. What interested (and perhaps disconcerted) Holmes the most in Harriman's essay, however, was the way in which he ended it: "Whether a person who makes a contract is bound to perform it, or whether he simply assumes the risk of having to pay damages, is an important question which will be discussed hereafter in connection with the subject of remedies for breach of contract."[13]

In Harriman, Holmes believed he had found a kindred spirit. Harriman, too, wanted to provide a pragmatic account of contract law. Notions that a legally enforceable promise turned on whether two individuals subjectively intended to agree with each other did not capture what the law did. Like the geologist trying to sort through rocks or the botanist looking for a way to classify flowers, legal scholars needed to discover the principles that accurately identified what actually happened when courts were called on to enforce contracts.

From Holmes's perspective, common law courts, when called on to enforce contracts, merely required the payment of money damages. Saying that a contractual obligation was an obligation to perform or pay money damages simply and completely described what courts did in contracts cases. Moreover, it forged a tight link between tort and contract liability.

The law of contracts could be organized around the idea that someone who entered into a contract was in the same position as someone who had committed a tort.[14] The tortfeasor, by acting negligently, became bound to pay a particular sum; a promisor, by making a promise, similarly bound herself to pay a particular sum. By driving negligently, I can be sued. If I make a promise, I open myself to a damage action if the promised performance does not take place. In the former case, I "commit" a tort. In the latter, I "commit" a contract. The only difference between the two is that the act that triggers the contractual obligation is subject to defeasance, while the act that triggers the tort obligation is not.

This is not, of course, the way ordinary individuals think about contracts. There are more flowery or elaborate or morally laden ways to describe a legally enforceable contractual obligation. In the end, however, such embellishments are unnecessary. All you need to say to capture the legal rule and predict what a judge will do in a particular case is that "a contract at common law is nothing but a conditional liability to pay damages, defeasible by performance."[15]

Holmes believed his account better than more elaborate accounts of contractual obligation, and he urged Harriman to adopt this view. It was to be preferred over other accounts because it was simpler.[16] When two theories explain as much, the better is the one that requires the fewest moving parts.[17] Injecting notions of morality or other ideas did no work. They had, again in the words of pragmatists Charles Sanders Pierce and William James, no "cash value."

Our neighbor plans on having a big party outside on Saturday. I promise to mow her lawn in exchange for $10. You promise, in exchange for $10, to cover her losses in the event that it rains on Saturday and the party has to be canceled. There are two variations on the facts to consider. First, I break my promise to mow the lawn, and our neighbor suffers damages as a result. In the other case, it rains and she is forced to cancel the party and asks you to honor your promise. How do we think about these two cases? Are they different from one another?

For purposes of everyday life, of course, the two situations are not at all the same. I made a promise and broke it; you provided insurance. But there is nothing from the judge's perspective that distinguishes the two cases. We share the same legal obligation. In both cases, our neighbor can come to court and force each of us to pay a compensatory sum. We are both obliged to pay because a promised event (mowing of the lawn or good weather) did not come to pass.

Harriman, however, rejected this account.[18] In his view, a legally enforceable promise contained both a primary obligation to keep the promise and a secondary obligation, in these cases the payment of damages, if one failed to keep the primary obligation. In some cases, the primary and secondary obligations correspond with each other. In the case of the promise to compensate our party giver if the sun fails to shine, "the primary obligation to compensate the other party for the non-occurrence of the promised event is necessarily coincident with the secondary or sanctioning obligation to pay damages for breach of contract."[19] But in other cases, the two do not correspond. When I promise to mow your lawn, there is a primary obligation—my obligation to mow your lawn—and a secondary obligation—to pay you damages if I fail to do so. As Harriman explained, "every breach of contract gives rise to a secondary obligation to pay damages; but in contracts where the thing promised is within the control of the promisor, there is, in addition, a distinct primary obligation to perform the contract."[20]

The private debate between Holmes and Harriman shows that the focus commonly put on Holmes's bad man and the law of contracts is misplaced. Holmes developed his "bad man" trope only because he failed in his initial effort to persuade Harriman that separating promises into primary and secondary obligations was not useful. He saw himself as the good teacher who tries a different explanation after the first fails. The bad man argument was in service of his effort to show a fellow pragmatist a simpler and therefore better way to think about contracts.[21] Without loss of generality, one could substitute "physicist" for "bad man."

Holmes and Harriman were both in search of general principles that would give a theory of contract analogous to the account scientists gave to the world around them. From Holmes's perspective, Harriman's account was flawed because it injected a concept—the distinction between primary and secondary obligations—that did too little work. In trying to account for what courts do, nothing is gained from distinguishing a promise to pay you if the sun does not shine from a promise to mow your lawn. The promisor has to pay a compensatory sum in both cases. Holmes took Harriman to task because his account added complexity without any corresponding benefit.

Harriman agreed that one should ask whether alternative accounts of contract law possess sufficient additional explanatory power to offset the additional complexity. Or, to put the same question differently, one should ask whether there are important ways in which Holmes's theory of contract damages fails to capture important features of the law.

Harriman argued that his distinction between primary and secondary obligations was useful.[22] It allowed one to distinguish between those cases in which specific performance was available and those in which only damages were available. In both cases, there was a primary obligation to perform, but in one instance the secondary obligation was to comply with an injunction, and in the other, the secondary obligation was to comply with an order to pay damages.

Holmes responded that there were "relatively few" cases in which equity responded with an injunction and noted, "I hardly think it advisable to shape general theory from the exception."[23] Therefore, he observed, "it would be better to cease troubling ourselves about primary rights and sanctions altogether than to describe our prophecies concerning the liabilities commonly imposed by the law in those inappropriate terms."[24]

Holmes, to some extent, misunderstood the challenge confronting someone searching for fundamental principles. To remain with the metaphor of the Young Astronomer, it is not enough to locate the various stars and planets. One must be able to single out the subtle ways in which observations depart from your theory and know whether these differences, regardless of how small they are, matter. The question again is not how much you miss but how important the missing elements are.

To be sure, Holmes's account of contract law corresponds in the main with the way contracts cases are decided. The typical remedy for a breach of contract is money damages. You catch most of the action when you center your theory of contracts around a damage action. But this is not the right question. We need to know whether the small deviations are significant. We need to know whether a theory of contract so centered on damages misses anything fundamental. Kepler observed the retrograde motion of Mars. It was only a small deviation from what Ptolemy's and Copernicus's model predicted, but it showed him that it was a mistake to think that the paths of heavenly bodies were circular. Orbits are elliptical. A theory that assumes that they are perfect circles is simply wrong.

The quiet and private debate between Holmes and Harriman during the 1890s focused on the question of who was providing the best theory, the theory that gave the better account of the law. The choice was between a straightforward one based on simply stated rules and a more nuanced one that looked behind them and set out a larger principle (the relationship between primary and secondary obligations).

Harriman tried to respond to Holmes's criticism of his work in the second edition of his book on contracts. Holmes's account of contract remedies can be squared with legal doctrine only when one limits it to common law causes of action. For Harriman this was contrary to the spirit of the pragmatist enterprise. An account of contractual obligation that ignored what happened before the chancellor was artificially truncated. Clients care about their obligations independent of which court happens to enforce them. No botanist would claim to have a theory if the theory were limited, by its terms, to yellow flowers. To give a scientific account of the law, one needed to provide a parsimonious explanation of the outcome of all cases.

Moreover, even with respect to common law courts, specific enforcement had a long history. Holmes's account neglected centuries of history. As Pollack and Maitland had pointed out, "[t]he oldest actions of the common law aim for the most part not at 'damages,' but at what we call 'specific relief.' "[25]

Harriman's next critique of Holmes went to the heart of the matter. Positing both primary and secondary obligations explained cases that Holmes's theory could not. Although not as simple, it did more work. Harriman used *Lingenfelder v. Wainwright Brewing Co.* to illustrate.[26]

An architect refused to turn over his plans for building a brewery as his contract required after he learned that the brewery would buy the refrigerating equipment for the plant from one of his competitors. The brewery needed the plant built immediately and so it agreed to increase the architect's fee to induce him to perform. When the architect came to collect the higher fee, the brewery refused to honor the revised bargain. The architect sued, and the court held that the promise to pay the additional fee was unenforceable. It was not supported by consideration.[27]

Holmes's account of contractual liability, one in which the promisor had a choice between performing or paying damages, could not explain such cases. By his account, the architect had a choice—to perform or subject himself to money damages. If he had a right to refuse to perform, then he could ask to be paid for not exercising this right of refusal. Giving up his right not to perform was consideration for the additional pay. Hence, under Holmes's account, the new deal, one in which the architect gave up his option to breach and performed instead, was supported by consideration. But the law is otherwise. It is standard blackletter that a promise to pay more for a performance already promised is not supported by consideration.

By contrast, Harriman could make sense of such a case. In his view, the architect's obligation to pay damages when he broke his promise was merely a secondary consequence of the primary obligation to keep the promise. The damages remedy was the way in which the law happened to enforce the primary obligation to perform. Liability for damages was distinguishable from the underlying obligation itself. Because the underlying obligation existed independent of the remedy, the promisor did not have an option not to perform. Hence, he gave no new consideration when he turned over the plans. There was no "option" for him to give up in return for the agreement to buy the refrigeration equipment.

This example shows how positing an underlying primary obligation has consequences independent of the sanction associated with the violation of the right. This decision, and others like it, could readily be explained by positing the existence of a primary obligation. Quarks cannot be seen, but there are some phenomena that can be explained only if they exist. Harriman's primary obligation is a legal analogue.

Though not noted by Harriman, conceiving the law of contracts as embodying a principle of primary obligation makes it possible to explain another important feature of contract law. The victim of a breach of promise possesses both a shield and a sword. In the face of a breach of promise, she can both sue for money damages and suspend her own performance. This ability is easier to explain with Harriman's account than with Holmes's.

Imagine that I promise to mow your lawn on Saturday morning, and in return, you promise to wash my car Saturday afternoon. As it happens, it is extremely easy for you to find someone else to mow your lawn but extremely hard for me to find someone else to wash my car. Saturday morning comes and I discover a more lucrative use of my time (mowing someone else's lawn, let us say), and so I breach. Long-established doctrine provides that our promises are mutual.[28] My breach releases you from your obligation to perform for me. You can refuse to wash my car. You are not liable for any damages from your refusal to keep your promise, no matter how easy it was for you to find someone to mow your lawn or how costly it would be for me to find someone to wash the car.

It is hard to reconcile this feature of the law with an account of contractual liability that gives the promisor the choice between performing and paying a compensatory sum. If there were no such thing as the existence of an underlying primary obligation and I possess an option to perform or not as I please, then it would seem that my breach would not affect your own option to perform or pay money damages. Of course, it is possible to restate Holmes's principle: The promisor has the obligation to perform or, in the alternative, pay money damages and lose the benefit of performance by the other party. But this reformulation is beginning to take us away from where Holmes started. Indeed, it shows how Holmes's understanding of the relationship between paying damages and performance is inverted. He claims that a contractual commitment is an obligation to pay damages subject to defeasance by the happening of a particular event (performance). But it is properly the other way around. Performance is the primary component of contractual obligation. Rather than merely calling off an obligation to pay money, performance is essential to securing the reciprocal part of the bargained-for exchange. Quite apart from any obligation to pay damages, you must perform in order to obtain performance in return.

More to the point, Holmes, like Harriman, is in search of the best and simplest explanation. The more epicycles one introduces into the mechanism, the worse it fares relative to rival accounts. Qualifications such as these, at least in any number, are exactly what Holmes cannot accept, given his own ambition to offer a parsimonious account of the law of contract. And this is not the end of the problems with Holmes.

Richard Epstein has identified another place where it is hard to reconcile the law with the idea that a contractual obligation was merely an option to perform or pay damages. Trustees and other fiduciaries are bound to maximize the value of the assets under their control. They do not have the discretion to give away assets or leave options unexercised. If the decision to perform a contract or breach were simply an option like any other, it would seem that the trustee should be obliged to exercise that option and breach any contract when it benefited the trust to do so. But this is not the law.

One should be cautious about giving Harriman too much credit. His analysis is thin, and his third and final rejoinder to Holmes (that "the doctrine involves an unreasonable departure by the law from fundamental ethical principles") is hardly illuminating.[29] Indeed, it is completely contrary to what Holmes expected to find in someone who seemed so in tune with his own agenda to provide a pragmatic account of the law.

There is another place where Harriman's theory of primary and secondary obligations does work. It is at the intersection of tort and contract. It may not loom large in terms of decided cases, but it may be, like the retrograde motion of Mars, a clue to seeing the principles at work in the law of contract.

Though he makes little use of it, the case is the first that Harriman cites in his chapter on remedies.[30] You hire me to sing at your opera house. Another impresario, knowing of the contract between us, persuades me to breach my contract with you and sing for him instead. He has a larger opera house and is able to put my talents to better use. In Holmes's world, there might be no particular enthusiasm for the rival impresario's actions, but the impresario has done nothing to which a judge need pay attention. I have an obligation to pay you money that I can defeat by performing. There is nothing independently actionable in my decision not to perform. Hence, there should be nothing wrong in the impresario persuading me not to perform.[31] The only consequence of my failure to perform is that my obligation to pay you money damages is not defeated.

But Holmes's account once again fails to give an accurate account of the law. *Lumley v. Gye* establishes that you have an action against the impresario in addition to an action against me. In Harriman's scheme, the existence of your action against a third party follows naturally from his distinction between primary and secondary obligations. You enjoyed a primary right to performance. Unlike an obligation to pay defeasible by performance, the right to performance can in principle give rise to multiple causes of action and against multiple people, quite apart from whether there is a damage action. As it happens, the law protects this right to performance both through a damage remedy and through an action against the person who induced the breach.

The action of tortious interference with contract can be justified precisely because of the existence of Harriman's primary obligation. The singer does not have an "option" to sing or pay damages. The first opera house has a right to her performance. The impresario commits a tort by inducing the singer to breach because the first opera house has a right to the performance, not just a right to damages that performance calls off. The impresario who induces the singer to breach interferes with this right.

Holmes's account of contract, and specifically his assertion that damages are the primary remedy, cannot explain tortious interference. The tort exists even when there might be a defense (such as one based on the Statute of Frauds) to the underlying cause of action.[32] Damages are available to capture the gains that the tortious interferer enjoys, even if they are greater than the expectation damages to which the promisee would be entitled.[33] Moreover, one can enjoin a third party from interfering with a contract, even though the promisee is entitled only to money damages from the promisor.[34] The contractual obligation to perform is at its heart a property rule. Although the property-like nature of the rule is typically beneath the surface, it exists nevertheless. Holmes's account of contract, centered as it is on money damages, cannot explain what is going on, but a property-focused theory of primary and secondary obligations can.

This suggests a radical reformulation of the law of contract.[35] To understand what a judge does in contract cases, we posit first that every legally enforceable promise comes with a primary obligation to keep the promise. Associated with this primary obligation is the remedy that the law attaches to the failure to do it. And the remedy in the first instance is a right to specific performance. The damages remedy, far from being an option available to the promisor, is the exception to the general rule. Again, this is the better view as a matter of history. To quote Pollack and Maitland again, "[t]he oldest actions of the common law aim for the most part . . . at specific relief."[36]

There are practical reasons not to award specific performance in the typical case. When contractual liability can be reduced to a sum certain, enforcement is straightforward. If the promisor fails to pay the judgment, the promisee can obtain a writ of execution and have the sheriff seize as much of the promisor's property as is necessary to satisfy the judgment. When it comes to paying a fixed amount of money, there is no doubt about what the promisor is obliged to do or whether she has done it. But if the promisor is ordered to mow the lawn or produce the wheat she promised, there is room for foot-dragging and substandard performance that invites further litigation. The promisee is no worse off with a damage remedy, and the burden on the court is considerably less.

In many cases, breach happens because it no longer makes sense for the promisor to perform. Family commitments unexpectedly take me out of town, and that is the reason I cannot mow your lawn as promised. Even if we had a regime of specific performance, we would bargain with each other in the shadow of the law. If the two of us were rational, you would agree not to exercise your right to specific performance, and I would pay you a fixed amount of cash. If cooler heads prevailed, the specific performance remedy would put us in the same place we would be in if there were a damage remedy in the first place.

Parties do not always behave rationally, and there is good reason to think that, after litigation, such negotiations will be costly and not always successful.[37] It may make sense to have damages as the typical remedy even if specific performance were conceptually what we were after. Damages reflect where we would end up if we both acted sensibly, even when there is a right to specific performance. As it gets us to this end point quickly, a damage remedy may be a sensible way to sidestep costly bargaining. Far from being the central feature of the law of contract as Holmes suggests, the damages remedy is simply a manifestation of a deeper underlying right premised on specific performance.

The question is how much to make of this critique of Holmes's account. Defenders of Holmes might well point out that tortious interference is a late arrival to the scene. The exceptions that require the most explaining live at the periphery of contract law. That Holmes's simple account does not capture all of contract is to be expected. In law, as in life, 95 percent is perfection.[38] But there is a different view. It is exactly at the periphery that we can see the difference between crude categories and fundamental principles. For the Young Astronomer, such things as the retrograde motion of Mars should not be glossed over. It is the difference between physics and stamp collecting.

4

The Expectation Damages Principle and Its Limits

Oliver Wendell Holmes and Richard Posner are the two dominant judge-scholars in the American legal tradition. They have much in common. They were born with a clear, effortless prose style that allowed them to capture subtle ideas with a few brushstrokes. Both enjoyed splendid liberal educations (at Harvard and Yale, respectively). Thereafter, each continued to read the classics (in their original languages) and remain in tune with the intellectual currents of their time. They served on distinguished law faculties (Holmes at Harvard; Posner first at Stanford, then Chicago) before going on to spend most of their careers on the bench. And, as scholars, each made his mark by producing a single volume that tried to make sense of the common law. The task was accounting for the outcome of discrete cases. What mattered was what courts did, not what they said. They devoted all their energy to giving an account of the heavens.

Like Holmes, Posner sought to reduce the common law to its core principles. For Posner, the basic postulates of microeconomics were what explained the essential features of the common law. The common law of torts turns on the idea of negligence because a negligence rule ensures that parties have incentives to take care.[1]

Grant Gilmore was Posner's colleague at Chicago while Gilmore was writing *Death of Contract,* and it is worth noting that his book concluded with this observation:

Perhaps we should admit the possibility of such alternating rhythms in the process of law. We have witnessed the dismantling of the formal system of the classical theorists. We have gone through our romantic agony—an experience peculiarly unsettling to people intellectually trained and conditioned as lawyers are. It may be that . . . [someone new] is already waiting in the wings to summon us back to the paths of righteousness, discipline, order, and well-articulated theory. Contract is dead—but who knows what unlikely resurrection the Easter-tide may bring.[2]

We do not know whether Gilmore was thinking of Posner, but Posner was indeed waiting in the wings as Gilmore wrote. In fact, his office was just a few feet away.

Holmes would have been sympathetic with Richard Posner's ambitious agenda in *Economic Analysis of Law*. It was the same agenda he had had in *The Common Law*: to lay out the basic principles of the common law in a single volume. Indeed, many of the attacks on Posner over the years have been of the sort that Holmes faced. The common law was too wonderful, and the law was too subtle to be reduced to the axioms of economics. Posner's account of the law was, like Holmes's, too remote, too detached, and too bloodless.

Perhaps Posner's most important contribution in contracts was to identify a singular virtue associated with expectation damages.[3] Posner set out with precision the "compensatory" sum that someone who breaches a contract must pay.[4] It is the amount that forces those who fail to keep promises to internalize the costs of breach. If the promisee had a right to full compensation for any harm she suffered in the wake of breach, the promisor would take account of the costs that her conduct imposed on others.[5] If the promisor still broke her promise, it would be because the social benefits of breach exceeded the social costs. If I have promised to mow your lawn on Saturday, but my talents are better put to use doing brain surgery, the world is better off if I breach. You can find someone else to mow your lawn, I can make you whole for any additional costs, and some third party's life will be saved. The rule, in addition to being simple, makes the world a better place.

When the law ensures that the innocent parties receive an amount equal to the value of their bargain, someone who makes a promise has no incentive to break the promise unless she has better opportunities elsewhere. And—this is the controversial point—if the potential contract breacher has better opportunities elsewhere, it is affirmatively desirable that advantage be taken of them. Holmes made no judgment about whether keeping a promise was good or bad; Posner appears to take the view that what he calls "efficient" breach is a good thing.[6]

The following example generally captures Posner's notion of efficient breach. I promise to mow your lawn on Saturday for $10. It will cost you $15 to have someone else do it, once the aggravation and inconvenience are taken into account. (We shall also assume that you would still pay to have your lawn mowed at $15 rather than do it yourself.) Posit now that some other opportunity comes my way.

If the two of us were cold-eyed and rational and if we could bargain costlessly with one another, I would end up not mowing your lawn if, but only if, I valued this other opportunity at more than $15. The legal rule makes no difference as long as the two of us are able to reach bargains that are in our joint interest. If the legal rule gave you the right to force me to mow your lawn, you would be better off releasing me from my promise as long as I was willing to pay you more than $15. You would rather have some amount more than $15 than have me mow the lawn, as you can hire someone else to do the same job with what I give you and still have money to spare. You would not take any less than $15, as it would leave you worse off than if you just insisted on performance. For my part, I will be willing to pay more than $15 to be released from my obligation only if I value my other opportunity as much. If I value the alternative opportunity at less than $15, I shall not be willing to pay you $15 in order to take advantage of it. The amount you need to be induced to release me from my promise is greater than what I am willing to pay.

We have the same outcome if the entitlements are allocated in exactly opposite fashion, and you have no ability to keep me from breaching at all. You will be willing to give me up to $15 to keep my promise. Doing this is better than the alternative of paying someone else to mow the lawn. You will not give me more than $15, because with this amount you can find someone else to do it. For my part, $15 will induce me to keep my promise only if again I value the other opportunity at less than $15. The flow of money changes with the legal entitlement but not the outcome. I shall still mow your lawn if, but only if, my other opportunity is something I value at less than $15.

We do not live in this counterfactual world of frictionless bargaining. The fact that we do not and that renegotiations are costly (and sometimes fail) provides a justification for expectation damages. A regime of expectation damages leads me to behave as I would if negotiations were possible and we could reach a deal with one another. If I must pay your additional costs to hire someone else at $15 in the event that I breach, I have no reason to breach unless I have an opportunity that brings me a benefit of more than $15. Even if bargaining is not possible, we still end up in the same place we would if bargaining were costless.

The expectation damages rule is thus uniquely sensible when transaction costs prevent renegotiation. If damages were less, I would have an incentive to breach even when my time was best spent mowing your lawn. If damages were greater, I would sometimes still mow your lawn, even though my time was better spent elsewhere. Only a regime of expectation damages ensures that the promise is kept if, and only if, keeping the promise remains mutually beneficial.

In putting forward this idea, Posner draws on the Coase theorem. Ronald Coase showed that in a world of frictionless bargaining, parties reach mutually beneficial bargains regardless of the legal rule. Posner believed that legal rules should be crafted with this baseline in mind. They should ensure the outcomes that parties would want if no negotiation barriers stood in their way. The basic principles of the common law were consistent with this idea.

The common law of contracts provides a sensible set of default rules that give most parties that for which they would bargain if they had the time and the money. We should not want things otherwise. A rule that, in the presence of bargaining costs, will induce me to mow your lawn when I have another opportunity I value at more than $15 ignores that we would find it in our mutual interest to change the outcome if we could. Similarly, a rule that leads me to break my promise when I value the alternative at less than $15 is similarly bad. My gain from breach is less than your loss. Breach is contrary to our joint interest.

To appreciate Posner's contribution to our understanding of contract, however, it is not necessary to accept the idea of efficient breach as morally attractive. Regardless of whether someone is morally obliged to keep her promises, there is a virtue in using expectation damages as the touchstone. This measure ensures that the promisor, when deciding whether to keep her promise, will take into account not only all the benefits of breach but also all the costs that the breach will impose on the other party. The rule has the effect of realigning incentives. When deciding whether to breach, the promisor in an expectation damages universe treats the costs her conduct imposes on others as if they were costs on her. Private and social costs are made equal.

One of the things legal rules can do is force people to internalize costs, and the prospect of having to pay expectation damages forces someone who contemplates breaking a promise to take account of the harm others will suffer in the event of breach. We see legal rules with this feature everywhere from tort law to the law of agency. The rule has the virtue of being informationally parsimonious. Awarding expectation damages does not require the court to measure the value to me of my alternative to mowing your lawn. The court needs to know only the cost to you of finding someone else to mow your lawn.

This rule, of course, does not overcome all our informational problems. Assume the contract involves my promise to sell you a machine that I own, and I decide to sell it to someone else instead because they are offering me more. In a regime of expectation damages, you are entitled to the amount that puts you in the same position. If a market value of the machine is not available, then the court must estimate the value that the machine would have had in your hands. This may be hard to do. It is, however, exactly in those cases in which it is hard to determine the buyer's benefit—when the goods are unique and cannot be readily replaced—that we typically do not have a rule of expectation damages but rather the remedy of specific performance.

The expectation damages principle provides us with a useful starting place. It sheds light on a variety of hard questions, beginning with the case of anticipatory damages, a subject to which I turn next.

Anticipatory Breach

Missouri Furnace Co. v. Cochrane illustrates the problem of measuring damages in the case of anticipatory repudiation.[7] The time is 1880. In early January, Cochrane promises to deliver 100 tons of coke to Missouri Furnace every working day of the year at a price of $1.20 a ton. There is a sudden rise in the price of coke in January, and Cochrane breaches the contract in mid-February. The challenge facing the court is determining the amount needed to compensate the promisee when the breach takes place before performance.[8]

In the wake of the breach, Missouri Furnace entered into a substantially similar contract with a different seller but at the much higher price of $4 a ton. This $4-per-ton price was less than the spot price for coke in February, and it was the prevailing price for a forward contract in February. The spot price of coke, however, later fell far below $4. If Missouri Furnace had waited and purchased coke throughout the year on the spot market, it would have paid on average substantially less than $4 a ton for its coke.

Missouri Furnace argued that the cost of entering the forward contract was the amount needed to make it whole. Later changes in the spot price were irrelevant. Cochrane took the opposite position. It argued that Missouri Furnace was taking its chances when it entered into another forward contract. In its view, Missouri Furnace was entitled only to the difference between $1.20 and the spot price for the coke at the time it was to be delivered throughout the course of the year.

The court agreed with Cochrane and held that Missouri Furnace was not entitled to recover for the costs of entering into the forward contract that subsequently proved unfavorable:

> [Missouri Furnace was] not bound to enter into such a contract, which might be to [its] advantage or detriment, according as the market might fall or rise. If it fell, [Cochrane] might fairly say that [Missouri Furnace] had no right to enter into a speculative contract, and [Cochrane might fairly] insist that he was not called upon to pay a greater difference than would have existed had [Missouri Furnace] held its hand. . . . As [Missouri Furnace] was not bound to enter into the new forward contract, . . . it did so at its own risk.

Our intuition tells us that there is something suspect about what the court is doing. The day before Missouri Furnace breached, it had Cochrane's promise to take care of all its needs for coke for the whole year in exchange for its promise to pay $1.20 a ton. After Cochrane breached, Missouri Furnace had to promise to pay $4 a ton to get someone else to promise to do the same thing—to satisfy its need for coke for the entire year. To put Missouri Furnace in the same position it had been in before Cochrane broke its promise, it would seem that Missouri Furnace needs damages based on the difference between $4 and $1.20.

Missouri Furnace entered into its contract with Cochrane in the first place because it had decided not to buy on the spot market. Missouri Furnace bargained for the benefit of a forward contract. Missouri Furnace did not want to buy on the spot market. It wanted to pay a fixed price for the coke. For that reason Missouri Furnace bargained for a forward contract with Cochrane, and it is this benefit that it lost when Cochrane broke his contract. To be made whole, Missouri Furnace needs the amount it would cost to enter into another forward contract.

In many cases, there will not be a forward market that the buyer can reenter. It may be much easier to figure out the spot price than the forward price. After all, once a spot-market rule is in place, Missouri Furnace can just buy coke in the spot market and send Cochrane the bill. It is not any worse off. Even if the forward contract measure is conceptually correct, is there anything the matter with the spot price measure? The price could prove higher or lower after the fact, but is there anything systematically wrong with it?

This question has an answer. The spot price measure is overcompensatory. Missouri Furnace is going to do no worse under a spot price measure than under the forward price measure, but it sometimes will do better.

Assume we use the spot price measure. If the seller breaches and the price of coke continues to go up, the seller takes the entire loss and the buyer is fully protected. The seller pays the difference between the contract price and the market price. This amount just gets bigger as the spot price of coke rises. The buyer ends up with the coal and is out of pocket to the same extent as if the promise had been kept.

But what if the price moves in the other direction? As soon as the spot price falls below the original contract price of $1.20, the buyer is better off than she would have been if the promise had been kept. In the absence of the breach, in the face of this decline, the buyer would have to buy coke at $1.20, a price that was greater than the market price. The seller's breach frees the buyer from this obligation. Under the spot price measure, the buyer remains protected if the price continues to rise but does not face the same costs when the price falls.

One can make the point with a simple example. On January 1, you promised to sell me coke at $15 for delivery on July 1, the prevailing forward price. It is now the end of February. You decide to retire, and you want to call off the contract. But since we entered into the contract, there has been labor unrest in the coke industry. Prices have risen, and I cannot find someone else who is willing to sell me coke on July 1 for $15.

Let us assume that, if the labor disputes are resolved and the workers enter a new contract, the price of coke will be $10 on July 1. But if things do not settle down, mines will shut down and the price of coke will be $30 on July 1. Either event is equally likely. These possibilities are reflected in the new forward price for coke of $20. ($20 is the average of $10 and $30.)

If you break your contract to sell me coke at $15, what damages should I recover? How much will it take to put me back into the same situation I was in before the breach? If others offer the same type of contract you offered me, I can simply enter into a forward contract. Because I have to promise this new seller $20 and I promised you only $15, I need $5 in damages to be made whole. (This $5 is the difference between the $20 market price and the $15 contract price.)

But what is my recovery if contract law gives me the difference between the spot price and the contract price? There is a fifty-fifty chance that the spot price will be $30. In that case, I shall buy for $30 on the spot market and send you a bill for the difference between $30 and the contract price of $15. If you refuse to pay, I have a damage action for $15.

Let us consider the other possibility. If the spot price drops to $10, it is below the contract price. I have not been injured by your breach. Indeed, you turned out to do me a favor by breaching. If I still want coke, I go out and get it for $10 instead of the $15 I would have had to pay you if you had not breached. I have no bill to send you, as I have not suffered any damages.

The average of these two possible events captures the expected value of the spot-market measure. This expected recovery of $7.50 (the average of $15 and $0) is greater than the $5 I would receive if the forward contract measure were in place. The innocent party receives more under a spot price measure than under the forward price measure. Because the forward price is enough to make the buyer indifferent to the seller's breach, the spot price measure is, in expectation, too large.

We should not rush to conclusions. A court might be justified in departing from the expectation damages principle in a case of anticipatory repudiation. The spot price may be readily ascertainable, and it may be a good approximation in cases in which the forward price is not available. The chance of the price falling below the original contract price may be small and the risk of overcompensation negligible.

Moreover, the cases when the forward price is unavailable may be the ones that matter the most. When the forward price is readily available, breach is less likely. A seller who wanted to retire could, instead of breaching, simply enter into the futures market and thereby find someone else to perform. She can take steps to minimize the risk she will have to pay too much.

The ease of getting spot price measures may outweigh the risk of overcompensation. We should not, however, do what the court did in *Missouri Furnace*. That court departed from the expectation damages principle without knowing it. If we depart from expectation damages, we should be aware of what we are doing.

The Hard Edges of Expectation Damages

The commitment to expectation damages is closely tied to the conception of contract that Holmes and his successors introduced. One either protects the promise, or one does not. One receives expectation damages, or one receives nothing. If I promise to mow your lawn in exchange for your promise to pay me $10 and then try to revoke the promise one minute later, you can sue me for the difference between what you would have to pay me to mow the lawn and what you must pay someone else to do it. I cannot say that you were not harmed or that you did not rely. As soon as I become bound, I have to give you the benefit of the bargain if I do not follow through. This feature of classical doctrine troubled Corbin and his contemporaries when they were pushing the boundary of what sorts of promises should be legally enforceable.

In 1926, during a meeting of the American Law Institute, Samuel Williston offered a variation on *Hamer v. Sidway*. Johnny tells his uncle he wants to buy a Buick, and the uncle says that he will give him $1,000. A prominent lawyer asked Williston whether, if Johnny then proceeded to buy a car in reliance on the promise for $500, the uncle would be liable for the full $1,000. Williston replied that Johnny should receive $1,000. As he explained, "Either the promise is binding or it is not. If the promise is binding, it has to be enforced as it is made." There might be an alternative theory of "quasi-contract" where the appropriate remedy would be the restoration of the status quo, but if the question was of enforcing the promise, it was a yes/no question.

For Williston and anyone else with a classical view, it makes no sense to provide less than expectation damages. One was either enforcing the promise, or one was doing something else. They rejected the idea that the promise could be incorporated into the fabric of the relationship between parties and that liability could emerge from the nature of the relationship rather than the existence of a promise per se. For the classically minded, the promise itself was reified. It becomes the object that is being protected.

If we gave you only a recovery for your out-of-pocket losses, we need not be that sensitive to when a legally enforceable promise comes into being. We could look at all the facts and circumstances and assess the reasonableness of your reliance, given my promises (and any ambiguity they might have contained). But when we require the breaching party to give the other the benefit of the bargain, the amount needed to put the innocent party in the same position that party would have been in had there been performance, we need to have rules that have hard edges to them.

Consider again *Flower City*. Although Flower sued the builder, it could have been the other way around. Imagine that it would cost the general contractor $125,000 to find someone to do the job that it thought Flower

City would do for $100,000. Imagine too that Flower thought that it was going to get a $25,000 profit from this deal. The next best job it could get if it did not have a contract to paint just the interior walls would bring it only $75,000, and it would incur the same expenses. If we say there is no deal, no one has to pay any damages. Conversely, if there is a deal and the deal is what the general contractor thought, it is entitled to $25,000; if there is a deal and the deal is the way Flower City says, then Flower City gets $25,000 instead.

If we lived in a world in which we awarded only reliance damages, it would not make any difference whether we found that the contract was to paint the interiors, that the contract was to paint everything, or that there was no contract at all. As long as the misunderstanding was discovered quickly, it would not take any money to restore things to the way they were before the contract was entered into. To be sure, both Flower and the builder are worse off than they thought they would be. Neither has the $25,000 gain it thought it would get. But neither may be any worse off as a result of entering into this deal.

Of course, we cannot be sure that one of the parties in *Flower City* did not incur costs in reliance on the bargain they thought they struck. The price of paint may have gone up or down after the deal and this would affect the contract price, regardless of whether the contract included the hallways. More likely, both Flower and the builder incur costs trying to find a new painter or landing a new job on a much shorter time fuse than is ordinary. But it is only if we are going to award expectation damages that the stakes become large.

Dramatic things happen in an expectation damages universe. If there is a contract, you get expectation damages. If there is not, you get nothing. Much turns on whether a contract is formed. For this reason, if you are a fan of expectation damages, you are also likely to be a fan of formal rules that make it easy to tell whether a contract exists.

The opposite applies if you are not a fan of expectation damages. We observe a correlation between a loose standards-based approach to contract formation and a reliance measure of damages. The more we think that we are dealing with inherently ambiguous situations, the more we may try simply to cut the baby in half. What we may be doing is removing from the field of negotiations contract law entirely. We have a death of contract in the sense that we abandon any use of legal forms to decide whether a contract comes into existence. Parties are simply to be guided by the mores of the commercial community in which they exist, and the legal rules will try to reinforce and vindicate the healthy ones. This kind of legal world is better for those who do not know the legal rules. They can act as if legal rules do not exist, because the legal rules simply track the customs that are around them. This is all to the good.

Contemporary contracts scholars are not likely to follow Williston and believe that sheer logic requires that promises be enforced or not. They recognize that fixing a particular moment of contract formation is sometimes artificial. They embrace the world of contract with its hard edges because, at least in the commercial context, it provides parties with a useful way to organize their affairs. Being able to make promises enforceable itself has value and having expectation damages as a starting place advances parties' mutual self-interest. We both are willing to subject ourselves to expectation damages because we each want the other to take our interests into account when tempted to breach. I want you to feel my costs when you breach, and you feel the same way about me.

The Overreliance Problem

Awarding expectation damages does not align incentives perfectly. The virtue of enforcing promises derives in large measure from allowing the other party to rely on the promise. But there can be too much of a good thing. Awarding the innocent party full expectation damages induces overreliance.

Let us assume that I am building a hotel and acting as my own general contractor. I expect to be finished by January 1, but I recognize that a delay of a week or more is possible. I start to book rooms and conventions in advance. The events for February or March require little reflection. They promise to be highly lucrative, and even if many things go wrong with construction, I am confident that the hotel will still be ready. But when it comes to two conventions in the month of January, the decision is harder.

I look at the numbers for the first January convention. Even if the hotel is finished on time, I shall end up losing a little money, so I decide not to book it. The numbers for the second January convention are more promising. If the hotel is completed on time, I stand to make a significant profit. But I need to worry about the possibility of delay. If some unusual event comes my way, I shall either owe a large amount to the disappointed conventioneers or be forced to incur enormous expenses to finish the hotel on the original schedule. I decide the risk is too great, and I do not book this convention either even though it would be profitable if everything were finished on time.

Consider now how my incentives change in an expectation damages world when I hire you to build the hotel for me, and you promise to finish by January 1. If you knew as much about the hotel business as I did, you would insist that I not book either of the January conventions. You do not have this expertise, however, and do not know enough to set out these limitations on my actions in our contract. The contract we have is imperfect, and I retain the ability to decide which conventions to book.

With your promise in hand, I think about whether to book the conventions differently. I treat the finishing of the hotel on schedule as a sure thing. You are obliged either to complete the hotel on time or to put me in the same economic position I would be in if you had. I still do not book the first January convention. I lose money on this convention regardless of whether you finish on time. Expectation damages gives me no incentive to engage in an activity that is inherently unprofitable. But the second convention is a different matter. I profit if you keep your promise and the hotel opens on schedule, and the prospect of expectation damages guarantees me the same profit even if you do not. I do not care if I have to cancel the convention, as you would make me whole.[9]

The effect of expectation damages is to make my profit from the second January convention certain. You are insuring me against delay. I no longer take into account the risks that would have kept me from booking this convention if I had been building the hotel myself. If the hotel does not open on time, I can shift onto you all the costs of dealing with disappointed conventioneers. Awarding expectation damages, as conventionally calculated, gives me an incentive to "overrely." I treat your performance as more certain than I would treat my own performance if I were building the hotel myself.

To understand this example, it is important to recognize that it is not simply a question of my benefiting at your expense. You may well demand a higher price in advance to compensate you for the expected losses from my overreliance and your inability to craft a contract sufficiently detailed to prevent me from overrelying. Quite apart from how the harm is allocated between us, we are jointly worse off than we would be in a world in which one person both built and ran the hotel. Given the risk, booking the second January convention exacts a social cost. Indeed, if the risk of overreliance were large enough, you might insist on being paid so much that it no longer made sense for me to have you build the hotel in the first place.

To ensure that we both have the right incentive, expectation damages should be reduced to the amount necessary to put me in the same position I would be in if I booked the same conventions I would have booked had I built the hotel myself. I should not recover for losses from the second convention even if you breach the contract. Such a rule, however, imposes enormous informational burdens on the courts. Instead of looking at my actual expenses, the court has to imagine my expenses in the counterfactual world in which I take account of the possibility that performance is not certain. A court has no easy way of knowing what conventions I would or would not be booking if I were the one who bore all the risk.

The problem of overreliance is not, however, a reason to prefer any of the commonly proposed alternatives to expectation damages. A regime of reliance damages, the amount necessary to return the parties to the same position in which they found themselves before the promise was made, induces overreliance as well. In the hotel example, I shall still book the second convention in January. (If the hotel opens on time, I enjoy the profits and I am better off. If it does not, I am no worse off. I do not recover the profits of the second convention from you, but you do pay for my out-of-pocket losses from having booked it.)

But under a reliance regime I may book the first convention as well. I shall still lose money on the first convention if you finish by January 1, but the extra damages you face if you do not finish on time makes you more likely to keep your end of the bargain. By increasing the likelihood you finish on time, I make it more likely I will enjoy the profits from the second convention. I care that you perform in a reliance-based regime because, unlike expectation damages, I am not fully compensated in the event of breach. The benefit from giving you an added incentive to perform may more than offset the cost to me of having one unprofitable convention.

In contrast to expectation damages, under a reliance-based regime I enjoy the profits on the second convention only if you finish on time. I am not indifferent to whether you perform or pay damages. I want you to perform. This is the only way I can profit from the second convention. I shall search for ways of imposing costs on you to give you an added incentive to finish on time. Booking the first convention in early January does this. The prospect that you will have to compensate me for not one but two groups of disappointed conventioneers will lead to you to move heaven and earth to finish on time. The small loss to me from the first convention may be worth incurring if it ensures you will finish on time and allow me to enjoy the profits on the second convention, profits I shall not receive if you breach.[10]

Hence, the award of reliance damages increases my incentive to act inefficiently relative to expectation damages. I shall book both January conventions rather than just one. Because of the overreliance problem, an expectation damages regime is unambiguously better than a reliance damages regime.

Overreliance and the Rule of *Hadley v. Baxendale*

Even though overreliance is not as big a problem in an expectation damages regime as in others, we still need to pay attention to it. There are a number of limitations on the expectation damages principle that partially respond to the overreliance problem. The most important of these is the rule of *Hadley v. Baxendale*.

Hadley ran a stream-driven mill in Gloucester in the 1850s.[11] As this was before the era of standardized parts, every part of the mill was custom-made. When the mill shaft broke, it needed to be shipped back to the manufacturer a hundred miles away. The manufacturer needed the broken mill shaft in order to have a template to make a new one.

Hadley contracted with Baxendale to transport the mill shaft to the manufacturer. Baxendale consolidated the mill shaft with a shipment of several tons of iron goods also bound for the same manufacturer. Instead of going by rail, this shipment was sent by canal, a slow mode of transportation on its way out at this time. Because of this delay, Hadley's mill was shut down for five days longer than expected.

This delay was a breach of contract, and Hadley wanted to recover damages for these five additional days. These were quite substantial. In addition to lost profits, Hadley had to buy flour from elsewhere to meet its various contractual obligations. Recovering the lost profits and these added expenses was necessary to put Hadley in the position he would have been in if Baxendale had kept his promise. But we have an intuition that recovery of such consequential damages does not make intuitive sense in cases where they are unusually large.

Take the following example.[12] You are Hadley's great, great grandson and you run a mill in downtown Chicago. The mill shaft breaks and it must be shipped back to Lisbon. The last plane for Lisbon leaves in twenty minutes. You grab the mill shaft and hail a cab. It is driven by

Baxendale's great, great granddaughter. You say, "I'll give you $20 extra if you promise me you to get me to the airport in twenty minutes." She responds, "Hop in, buddy." You get caught in traffic. Notwithstanding her heroic efforts, you miss the plane. She agreed to get you to the airport in twenty minutes, and she failed to do so. Like Baxendale, she broke her promise. Most of us share the intuition that the cab driver does not have to pay for your lost profits even though she would if there were no qualification to the expectation damages rule.

Hadley v. Baxendale adjusts the expectation damages principle and reflects the intuition that the cab driver should not be tagged with full expectation damages. This is a case where you are able to minimize losses (everything from having a backup mill shaft to leaving for the airport a few minutes earlier), and the cab driver has relatively fewer steps she can take to ensure that she gets to the airport on time.

The rule of *Hadley v. Baxendale* has two parts. Its first part provides that Baxendale is liable only for those damages that arise "naturally" or "in the usual course of things." Baxendale is not liable for Hadley's actual damages when they are unexpectedly large. If there are "special circumstances" and Hadley says nothing, he remains at risk. The idea is that as soon as there is something unusual about Hadley's likely damages, he has to do something about it. He cannot fall back on the expectation damages principle and overrely. This part of the rule of *Hadley v. Baxendale* reduces the problem of overreliance by taking those people who are different from the norm out of the expectation damages universe.

The judges in the case intuited that there was something fundamentally wrong about sticking with the idea that the breaching party should be liable for all the damages that flow from breach. But this first part of *Hadley* is not obviously right. This effort to check Hadley's incentive to overrely comes at the cost of giving Baxendale too little incentive to take care. Baxendale will know that he never pays more than actual damages and sometimes he will pay less. Hence, on average, he will pay less. If he pays less in expectation than his customers lose when he breaks his promise, then he will not fully internalize the cost of failing to keep his promises.

But there are reasons for thinking that the basic rule makes sense. You worry about proof problems if damages awards are too high. You also worry that to the extent damages are high, Hadley is best positioned to avoid them. Moreover, the rule does not forbid Hadley from getting expectation damages. He can still bargain for them. The rule is simply that he must negotiate a special deal when his circumstances are unusual. If you are an outlier, you have to identify yourself. By giving unusual parties less than their damages, the rule induces them to reveal that they are special. *Hadley v. Baxendale* is consistent with the idea that contract law not only allocates risk but also provides the starting place for parties to negotiate with each other.[13]

The first part of *Hadley* is as rock solid a legal principle as you can find in the law of contracts. A party is not entitled to recover all consequential damages that flow from a breach of contract but only those that are reasonably foreseeable. The basic contract damages remedy differs from tort damages (and is generally more expansive) because, rather than restoring things to the way they were before the fact, it focuses on the benefit the promisee would have received had there been full performance. The "reasonably foreseeable" test that is the distinctive feature of *Hadley* pulls in the opposite direction.

In tort, if you are liable, you are liable for all damages proximately caused by your negligence. While you are on vacation, I negligently drive onto your lawn and sever your water main. Your exotic orchids drown. I am liable for the full cost of the orchids, no matter how rare and unusual they are. In contract, I am liable only for the damages that are reasonably foreseeable. I promise to water your garden while you are on vacation. I not only water it but flood it. Your flowers die. I am liable only for the damages that you would have if you had an ordinary garden. If your flowers are unusually valuable, you have to tell me.

There is a second part to *Hadley* that is more troubling. Under it, all that Hadley needs to do to return to a full expectation damages universe is to tell the other party of the likely consequences of breach. Once informed, Baxendale has to dicker if he does not want to assume liability. It is not obvious why the mere fact of communication should be all that Hadley needs to do to shift the baseline back to expectation damages. This returns us to the hop-in-buddy problem.

Consider the same example with Baxendale's great, great granddaughter, but this time Hadley's great, great grandson tells her his situation: "If I can't get this mill shaft to the airport in twenty minutes, the mill will be shut down for an extra day, and I will lose $20,000 in profits. Can you get me to the airport in time? I'll give you $20 extra if you promise me you can." She again responds, "Hop in, buddy." He still misses the flight.

On its face, the second half of *Hadley* provides that merely providing information is sufficient to shift liability. Once told about the lost profits if Hadley's great, great grandson misses the flight, the cab driver is liable for the full loss. Our intuition tells us that liability should not be shifted so easily. There are many reasons. In an industrialized economy, the person who is given the relevant information (e.g., the clerk in the shipping office) may not even have the power to make a special deal. Baxendale is unlikely to give his agent this kind of power. Second, there may be some ambiguity about what is actually said. In the case itself, we do not know if the agent was told that the mill would be shut until a new shaft could be made. Third, if we want to make it easy for parties to roll their own deals, it is bad for the background rules to turn on acts that the parties themselves do not know have legal consequence. The effect of such rules is to impose liability on those who are not skillful enough to disclaim.

That *Hadley* does not go far enough in limiting the expectation damages principle has long been apparent. Holmes himself made an effort to cabin the second part of *Hadley* by introducing what has come to be known as the "tacit agreement test" in *Globe Refining:*

> The extent of a promisor's liability in contract cases is likely to be within his contemplation, and, whether it is or not, should be worked out on terms which it may fairly be presumed he would have assented to if they had been presented to his mind.

In all cases, we should try to flesh out the terms of the implicit bargain. We should try to imagine what the fully dickered contract between you and the cab driver would look like. The most natural understanding of the interaction is that the $20 is a bonus for the cab driver. You must pay her the metered rate regardless, but if she fails to get you to the airport on time, she does not get the extra money. Virtually every carrier (including Federal Express) disclaims liability for consequential damages for delay, regardless of notice. This nearly universal practice between sophisticated parties suggests that the second half of *Hadley* cannot be a sensible default rule. There is no reason to think a random cab driver would accept an obligation that FedEx categorically refuses, and it makes little sense to impose it on her merely because information is conveyed to her.

There is another way to think about this problem that leads to the same conclusion. A contract that gives Hadley full expectation damages can be seen as two separate contracts. One is a contract to ship the goods, and the other is a contract of insurance protecting Hadley in the event that the shipment takes longer than expected. It is not plausible to assume that Baxendale would agree to issue this insurance policy to anyone who asked for it. Hence, merely notifying Baxendale about special needs should not suffice. The tacit-agreement test seems consistent with a view of contract that is based on the idea of consent.

In the hop-in-buddy example, one might remove some of the pressure from the second half of the *Hadley* rule by finding that the driver promised only to use her best efforts to get to the airport in twenty minutes. If she uses her best efforts, there is no breach, even if her fare misses the flight. This takes care of a substantial part of the problem but does not entirely solve it, as we likely think that she would still not agree to pay full expectation damages in those situations in which her passenger could persuade a jury that she failed to use her best efforts.

In the end, the issue is ultimately one of deciding who has the burden of calling off the background rule. Courts have generally not followed Holmes's lead explicitly. Judges nominally accept both parts of the rule of *Hadley v. Baxendale* and have not adopted the tacit-agreement test.[14] But if you look more closely, you will see that a number of qualifications on the second part of *Hadley* have grown up over time. These qualifications lack theoretical coherence, but they leave us in much the same place as if the tacit-agreement test were the law. When Hadley puts Baxendale on notice, Baxendale does become liable for the reasonably foreseeable damages that flow from the new circumstances, but only if they can be calculated with certainty and only if Hadley could not have avoided the damages. There is also the suggestion that Baxendale's damages cannot be grossly disproportionate to the amount he was paid to transport the mill shaft. These qualifications put together generally solve the hop-in-buddy problem in generally the same way as the tacit-agreement test.

The rule of *Hadley* is one sort of modification to expectation damages that Holmes and Posner fold into their approach to contract damages. It does not represent a fundamental challenge to their using expectation damages as the starting place. Such a challenge, however, is possible even when one accepts the idea that the promise itself should be point of focus and promissory liability should be an objective, on/off affair.

Expectation Damages and Option Pricing

The justification for expectation damages rests on the idea that we need to give the party contemplating breach the right set of incentives. It is not obvious, however, that this should be our primary focus to the exclusion of other goals. Indeed, as we have noted, we need to worry about these incentives only to the extent that there are barriers that keep the parties from renegotiating with each other.[15]

Suppose you promise to sell me a machine for $1,000 that will give me $200 in additional profit. Before you deliver it to me, you find someone for whom it will generate $500 in additional profit. It might seem that a damage rule allowing you to breach your contract with me and pay me $200 is better than a specific performance remedy. After all, the third party values the machine more than I do. But things are not so simple. Instead of using the machine myself, I might have sold it to the same third party who values it so much more than I do. A specific performance regime would lead to the same outcome as expectation damages. More to the point, once you find the other buyer, you can always renegotiate with me. I should be willing to release you from your promise for some amount between $200 and $500. The machine will end up in that person's hands regardless of what the damage remedy is.

Posner's justification for expectation damages rested crucially on the assumption that such renegotiations were hard. But this is only an assumption. If the costs of renegotiation are low, we need to worry less about forcing you to internalize the costs of breach. We may want the legal rules to ensure that other incentives are properly aligned.

Among other things, we want to ensure that the opportunities to put the machine to its best use are not neglected. After you and I enter into a contract for the machine, but before it is delivered, there is a chance someone else whom neither of us has found values it more. Assume that it costs $40 to run an advertisement that has a one-in-ten chance of locating a buyer who will pay an additional $500 for the machine. Running the ad makes sense under these assumptions. It has an expected value of $10, the difference between the advertisement's cost and its expected return (a one-in-ten chance of $500, or $50).

In a regime of expectation damages, however, neither you nor I will run the advertisement. You will not run the advertisement because you will capture only $300 of the $500 extra that the third party will pay. (You must pay me $200 in expectation damages.) Looking for a third party to buy the machine brings you an expected benefit of only $30. This does not justify a cost of $40. For my part, I have even less of an incentive to run the advertisement. Making the buyer aware of the machine will lead to your selling that person the machine instead of me. Expectation damages makes me whole, but I enjoy none of the benefit of finding someone who values the machine more than I do.

By contrast, a rule of specific performance gives me the incentive to run the advertisement. Once we enter into the contract, I shall act as if I own the machine. Because I can force you to give me the machine for the contract price, I enjoy the entire upside. I shall be willing to spend the $40 on the advertisement. By giving me a remedy of specific performance, I have from the time of the contract the incentive to spend the resources necessary to ensure that the machine is put to its highest valued use, whether it is in my hands or someone else's.

Of course, if we had all the time and money in the world, we would agree in our contract to run the advertisement and set out exactly how much you owe me in the event that the third party appears. But the cost of writing such a contract is high. Indeed, it is this sort of cost that is supposed to drive our choice of default rules. Insisting on expectation damages creates an environment in which neither one of us enjoys all the incentives that someone who owned the machine outright would have. Neither of us will be on the alert for others who valued the machine more than either of us does.

In short, a regime of expectation damages is imperfect. Of course, every default rule has its deficiencies, but we should not accept expectation damages uncritically. A still more radical critique of expectation damages is possible. Why is the cost that breach will impose on the innocent party the baseline that we think parties would themselves find in their mutual interest? I promise to mow your lawn on Saturday. If we negotiated over the matter explicitly, how much would we agree I should have to pay you if I decided not to perform? To be sure, forcing me to internalize the costs of breach is one of the factors that we would take into account, but it is hardly the only one, and it is not obvious that it should dominate.

Indeed, we see a number of environments in which parties negotiate over such matters explicitly. Parties sometimes enter into a deal and explicitly bargain for a right to cancel. It is called a "bust-up" or "break-up" fee. In return for paying a fixed sum, I can walk away from my contract with you. The amount that needs to be paid is the subject of explicit negotiation, and this amount tends not to look anything like expectation damages.

Parties might want something other than expectation damages because of the way another remedy allows parties to convey private information. A widow wants to ensure that a monument to her husband is built before she dies.[16] Her health is uncertain and her children untrustworthy. One of the potential suppliers of the monument might offer to pay an amount that greatly exceeded expectation damages as a way of signaling its reliability. This supplier can distinguish itself from others by agreeing to pay a penalty instead of damages. The widow can infer that this supplier is better able to deliver the tombstone on time because it is willing to take a huge hit if it does not and no one else is. A penalty clause works as an effective signal because anyone who is not reliable goes broke if they try to send it. The common law's antipathy to penalty clauses may be a mistake, at least in environments such as this one in which the risk of advantage taking is not present.

One can use artificially low damages to convey information as well. I promise to paint your portrait. I want to convey to you that I shall do a good job. I give you the right to walk away from the contract in return for paying me a nominal sum. I open myself to some opportunism. You will not take account of all my costs in deciding not to buy your portrait. Nevertheless, such an undercompensatory measure may be in our mutual interest as it gives me a way to signal that I shall devote my energies to doing a portrait that suits your tastes.

Of course, one can argue that if we explicitly allow a party to back away under specified conditions, then there is no breach. We can say that the contract includes a right to cancel. The party in exercising the contractually granted option is not breaching. But in the Holmesian universe, this should not matter. The option to pay damages is merely one additional term. There is no special magic attached to breach in this world. Our default terms include an option to cancel in every contract and the damage measure is simply the price of exercising that option to cancel.

In short, the link between the conception of contract as the right to perform or pay compensatory damages is not as tight as it might seem. There is still much work that remains to be done. Contract law operates in a world in which there are many other forces at work—such as custom and reputation. It is one thing to understand the effects that different rules of contract damages have. It is quite another to understand how these rules interact with other forces at work in a contractual relationship.

5

Terms of Engagement

The law of contract needs to give parties a set of background rules against which they interact. When two merchants meet and begin to bargain, both are better off when there is a sensible set of ground rules that both understand. Recall the scene in *Butch Cassidy and the Sundance Kid*. Harvey, a tall, strong, and rather stupid man, decides to contest Butch's leadership of the Hole-in-the-Wall Gang. Harvey insists that the leadership question be settled with a knife fight. He draws his knife and is prepared to fight. Butch approaches him unarmed and, waving his arms, says "No, no. Not yet. Not until me and Harvey get the rules straightened out." A dumbfounded Harvey drops his guard and exclaims, "Rules? In a knife fight? No rules!" At this point, Butch, still approaching and still unarmed, kicks him in the groin. While Harvey is writhing in pain on the ground, Butch announces, "Well, if there are no rules, let's get the fight started." He then takes one more swing at the now helpless Harvey to secure the outcome. Butch retains control of the gang without ever touching a knife or, by the standard Harvey unwittingly set, fighting unfairly. The lesson, of course, is that background rules are needed with respect to every agreement, even an agreement to settle a dispute with a knife fight.

Good Faith

Virtually every legal system assumes that, at a minimum, merchants cannot affirmatively lie to each other. But this leaves much about the ground rules unclear. At the outset, we need to know something about the language of the relevant merchant community to know what counts as a lie. In a Turkish bazaar, a merchant offers another $15,000 for a piece of jewelry. The second merchant replies that he promised his dying mother that he would not sell it for less than $20,000. To take a penny less would dishonor her memory. He starts to walk away. When the first merchant then counters with $17,500, the second merchant's concerns about his mother's honor suddenly disappear. He quickly turns back and accepts.

This merchant did not lie when he said that taking less than $20,000 would dishonor his late mother. To be sure, his mother, far from being dead, is in robust health and has never heard of the jewel, but the statement was a lie only if the first merchant believed it, and he did not. If he were the sort of person who did, he would not be trading in a Turkish bazaar, at least not for long.

A number of years ago, there was a television commercial in which Spike Lee insisted that Michael Jordan played basketball as well as he did only because of the shoes he wore. Anyone who bought the same shoes would play equally well. It was not true, but again there was no misrepresentation. For something to be a lie, it has to be believed and relied on.

The more common problem arises not when someone is affirmatively dishonest but rather when one chooses to look the other way. Obi-Wan Kenobi tries to charter a ship so that he and his companions can escape capture from the authorities. The ship captain asks him to identify the cargo, and he replies, "Myself, the boy, two droids, and no questions." With this information in hand, the ship captain does not actually know that he is participating in something illegal. But can the captain continue as if everything on this voyage were on the up and up? To what extent is a manifest that lists "myself, the boy, two droids, and no questions" sufficient to require the captain to ask more questions or lose his claim of innocence with respect to the enterprise?

We want people to be honest, but we cannot condition every commercial deal on each merchant stopping to investigate when anything appears unusual. Nor can we count on a court being able to sort through all of this after the fact.

In 1835, speculation in land in Maine was the coming thing.[1] Two suspect characters, men named Keith and Norton, found a parcel of land that was owned by some Europeans. The agent of the Europeans agreed to sell the land, provided Keith and Norton could come up with the financing. Keith and Norton persuaded a number of investors, including George Tysen, a New York merchant, to come into the deal. Tysen and the others would pay for the land in four annual installments. Keith and Norton told them that they already owned the land at the time they got these commitments, even though they did not own the land and never would.

The next year Keith and Norton returned to New York. They collected the second installment, the one that is at issue in this case, in the form of a bill of exchange, a draft, drawn by Norton and Keith on Tysen in favor of Norton and Keith. Tysen then accepted this draft (probably by signing on the front of it). The effect of this arrangement is to create a negotiable instrument on which Keith and Norton, as well as Tysen, are liable. The piece of paper that Tysen signed, a bill of exchange, was valuable in the hands of Norton and Keith because Tysen was creditworthy. Someone would pay for this piece of paper, independent of the creditworthiness of Norton and Keith, because Tysen was liable on it as well. Moreover, Tysen's liability on the instrument is independent of whether Norton and Keith were in breach of their obligations to him. From Tysen's perspective, signing the negotiable instrument was nearly tantamount to giving Keith and Norton cash.

It turns out that at the time they obtained Tysen's signature, Keith and Norton were already insolvent. They may have been trying to put together some kind of deal that would pull them out of the fire. We do not know. But they had lots of other trouble, quite apart from having lied to Tysen and the other investors about owning the land. Among other things, they had themselves drawn a draft on their own bank in Portland, Maine, that came due at about this time.

We do not know exactly what happened at this point. Swift, the cashier at the bank, reported that through his own inadvertence the draft went unpaid and when this was called to his attention, he paid the draft himself. He then went to Keith and Norton and asked that they repay him. They were short on cash, but they did have the negotiable instrument Tysen had signed. They gave this to Swift to make him whole. A little while later, they disappeared for the West.

Keith and Norton, of course, had no rights against Tysen. They were subject to any defenses that Tysen had against them, and these were many (starting with fraud). But Swift could pursue Tysen free of these defenses, provided that Swift had acted in "good faith" when he acquired the note. Swift had been objectively honest, but the transaction was irregular. One can take the view that when Keith and Norton appeared on his doorstep with their bags packed, Swift should have been more suspicious. He acquired the note, it might be argued, only because of his willingness to look the other way.

The case ultimately reached Joseph Story on the Supreme Court. Justice Story did not linger over the question of whether Swift acted in "good faith."[2] Nothing in the record suggested that Swift had any actual knowledge of wrongdoing, and for Story this was enough. He took the view of "good faith" commonly known as the rule of the "pure heart and the empty head." As long as you are honest in fact, you act in good faith. As long as you are not informed about the particulars, you can carry suspicious passengers who insist that no questions be asked.

Joseph Story's approach emphasizes the importance in commercial law of keeping the rules and boundaries clear. A question such as whether one acted in good faith ought to have a yes/no, on/off character that is not subject to after-the-fact weighing of the facts and circumstances. It is much better to expose someone like Tysen to the risk of loss than to make it uncertain where people stand. We should not put too much faith in the ability of judges or juries to assess after the fact exactly what kinds of inquiries merchants should make under each set of circumstances.

A standard of good faith that examined Swift's actions more closely would not merely make life awkward for ship captains who had few scruples about smuggling. It would prevent merchants from going forward with transactions any time something fell outside the ordinary. They would have to take on a burdensome inquiry, and even that might later be found to be insufficient.

Joseph Story's view did not prevail in the end. Those responsible for reshaping commercial law in the twentieth century—principally the legal realist Karl Llewellyn—believed that judges were able to access the norms of merchants.[3] There are norms of fair dealing in the trade. Reputable merchants do not look the other way. There are terms on which they will not do business. We can rely on these to provide objective measures of good faith. Your good faith can be questioned if you engage in a transaction that would have given others pause. You lose the right to assert your good faith even if you have no knowledge of the fraud, as long as you were told enough that would put a reputable merchant on notice that something was amiss.

A case illustrates how this test of good faith operates.[4] The story begins with a cheerful and perhaps somewhat liquored investor at a Wall Street holiday party. The investor mentions casually (and happily) to a managing director of an investment bank that he invested in a particular fund and that it was up 20 percent for the year. This strikes the managing director as decidedly curious. He knows this fund used his bank's prime brokerage services, and it had lost nearly $180 million over the previous twelve months. The director is sufficiently troubled that he goes back to his colleagues, and they conduct further inquiries. They contact the fund manager. The fund manager explains that their bank was only one of a number of prime brokers that the fund used and that, although investments done through their bank had done badly, others were doing well.

Neither the director nor the investment bank goes much further than this for a time. The explanation, though bogus, is not completely implausible. No one argues that the investment bank knew about the fraud. But the defrauded investors of the fund argue that, once the investment bank had this information in hand, it no longer possessed "good faith" in the modern sense. The comment at the holiday party was sufficient to raise suspicion. Those at the bank did some work to allay this suspicion but not enough.

The law gives a defrauded investor the right to recover money a con artist transfers to others if those receiving it do not act in good faith even if they give value in return.[5] Whether the investment bank here acted in good faith is a question of fact that a jury must resolve.

Defenders of the modern conception of good faith argue that such a factual inquiry is exactly what is necessary to distinguish those who follow the norms of the trade from those who engage in sharp practices.[6] In the typical case in which good faith is brought into question, the merchant has done a bit too well. The merchant has been paid a little too handsomely for the services offered. Those who receive too-good-to-be-true returns should not be surprised to have their good faith questioned. But the doctrine applies equally in cases in which the person who should have done more diligence does business with suspicious characters on ordinary terms.

Courts will typically apply some amorphous, multifactored test,[7] but one should not get caught up in such laundry lists. One should use common sense instead.[8] One cannot turn a blind eye after one comes to the point where one has seen enough to arouse suspicion. The principal issue in the good faith inquiry—and it is largely a factual inquiry—is identifying this point. The objective benchmark of good faith turns on reasonable standards of the relevant trade. A hedge fund is held to the reasonable standards we associate with other hedge funds. They should be more keenly aware of suspicious patterns (such as steady earnings year in and year out) than an amateur.

The uncertainties associated with an open-ended inquiry into good faith are exactly what led Justice Story to press for a test that required only absence of knowledge. Fraudulent schemes by their nature lack substance and cannot withstand close scrutiny. Hence, to be successful for any significant period of time, con artists need to convince investors that close examination is not feasible. They might, for example, tell them that making the details available to investors would reveal proprietary information. The more convincing the explanations the investors are given for not looking closely, the harder it is to question the good faith of the transferees.

After the fact, of course, fraudulent schemes seem silly. But when a con artist is able to amass large amounts of capital over a significant period of time and yields very good but not extravagant returns, it is easy to trust the track record and not look deeper. There are legitimate funds that do in fact bring substantial above-market yields. It seems a dangerous business for courts to sort between schemes that investors should identify as scams from those that are legitimate, especially as trading strategies become increasingly complex. If a fund can attract hundreds of millions of dollars over a period of many years, it seems doubtful a judge or jury is well equipped after the fact to identify those who should have asked more questions and those who were innocent victims.

It is worth underscoring that the investment bank in our case prevailed in the end. A jury found in its favor.[9] But defenders of Justice Story would argue that the investment bank should have been able to act as it did without being exposed to many years of litigation and the uncertainties associated with a jury trial. A commercial actor should not have to worry that her actions will be tainted because she failed to investigate rumors heard at a holiday party with sufficient care.

Of course, we do not want to allow people to get away with fraud. We should not reward bad faith. Fraud is never good, and we do not think rational people would strike a bargain with each other to the effect that they were allowed to cheat one another if they could get away with it. But the benefits of imposing a duty of inquiry needs to be weighed against the costs associated with a necessarily imperfect exploration of the facts and circumstances.

When you go to a holiday party under existing law, you not only need to ask yourself whether it makes sense to follow up on what you hear but also whether you will be exposed to liability if you do not. In addition, we have to worry about the cases we do not see—those in which an honest merchant cannot do business with another honest one because enough is out of the ordinary that one or the other thinks moving forward requires incurring too much legal risk.

Duty to Disclose

Even after we impose a general duty of good faith, much remains unclear. One can be acting in good faith and have no knowledge of any wrongdoing and still possess information that the other party would like to know. It is easy to see that we do not want a universal duty to disclose. In such a world, no one searches junk shops for hidden treasure. A valuable antique table ends up as a workbench in someone's garage instead of a museum. The need to reward those who gather information limits the amount of disclosure that we can require.

Chief Justice Marshall's opinion in *Laidlaw v. Organ* provides the baseline. Although everyone must act in good faith and refrain from any misrepresentations, there is no general duty to disclose. The dispute in *Laidlaw* arose in New Orleans in 1815. Because of the War of 1812, there was a naval blockade that had prevented raw goods from being shipped abroad. Prices would remain depressed until hostilities ceased. The United States had signed a peace treaty with Great Britain at the end of 1814, but news traveled slowly and the conflict continued. Andrew Jackson won the battle of New Orleans and occupied New Orleans. He continued to harass the British as they retreated, and he had also sent emissaries to negotiate the exchange of prisoners of war and the return of escaped slaves.

News of the treaty (and the prospect of an immediate lifting of the blockade) reached New Orleans in the middle of February. Among the first to obtain it was Organ, and he sought to take advantage of it. Shortly after sunrise on a Sunday morning, Organ bought a large amount of tobacco from an agent of Laidlaw. The agent asked whether Organ had heard any news that might affect the price, and Organ never answered the question. The news became generally available later that morning, and the price of tobacco immediately jumped 30 to 50 percent. Laidlaw refused to deliver the tobacco.

One can argue that the effort Organ spent finding the information (putting aside for the moment how he discovered it) is not something we particularly want to encourage. Getting advance word on a Sunday morning that a blockade is about to be lifted allows Organ to become richer at Laidlaw's expense, but it does not make the world a much better place. It is not like finding a museum piece otherwise destined for a garage. The best defense of the outcome of a case like *Laidlaw* is a familiar one. We cannot expect the law to be too finely tuned. We do not want judges or juries engaged in the business of determining after the fact whether the knowledge gained was socially valuable or not.[10]

In all events, blackletter contract law draws a sharp distinction between the buyer who possesses knowledge and remains silent and the buyer who possesses knowledge and who engages in deliberate misrepresentations. *Laidlaw v. Organ* tells us that the duty to disclose is modest in an arm's-length deal between merchants. As Justice Marshall explained:

> The question in this case is, whether the intelligence of extrinsic circumstances, which might influence the price of the commodity, and which was exclusively within the knowledge of the vendee, ought to have been communicated by him to the vendor? The court is of opinion that he was not bound to communicate it. It would be difficult to circumscribe the contrary doctrine within proper limits, where the means of intelligence are equally accessible to both parties. But at the same time, each party must take care not to say or do any thing tending to impose on the other.[11]

One should not, however, draw from this the inference that such a regime of nondisclosure is optimal. The common law provides one baseline, but there are others. As observed at the outset of this chapter, there must always be terms of engagement. Whether one is a merchant who seeks to sell wool in the twelfth century or a farmer who wants to sell grain in the nineteenth, regulations are inevitable, and these commonly include disclosure duties. The law merchant required goods sold at fairs to be openly displayed. The Chicago Board of Trade is the paradigm of a free market, and it is also among the world's most heavily regulated. Its elaborate rules establish who can trade, what can be sold, when trading can occur, and under what terms, and they include disclosure obligations as well.[12]

Trade-offs are inevitable. If there is information that parties to a trade commonly demand, it might make sense to require its disclosure. The alternative is to force parties to ask for this information and then, given the prohibitions from lying, draw inferences from silence if the other party refuses to provide it. Put in place too few disclosure obligations, and those who trade are forced into endless games of twenty questions.

There is much information in possession of the seller that sophisticated buyers insist on knowing before they are willing to trade.

On the other side of the coin, sellers will not answer every question, and sophisticated buyers will not insist on it. Too many disclosure obligations discourage traders from gathering information.[13] Everyone suffers because the prices do not take account of the information and thus do not reflect the underlying value of the asset. Perhaps because of this tension, clear benchmarks have not emerged.[14]

Consider the following case: Geologists for a mining company discover a vast mineral deposit on farmland in Canada.[15] After the discovery, the company decides to repurchase a large amount of its own stock. Two disclosure issues present themselves. First, does the mining company have to disclose the existence of the mineral deposits to the Canadian farmers when it seeks to acquire the mineral rights? Second, does the company have to disclose the existence of the mineral deposits to the Wall Street investors when it tries to repurchase its own stock?

The answer to both questions under existing law is plain. The firm is free to hire intermediaries and buy up the mineral rights from the naive farmers without disclosure as long as there are no lies or misrepresentations.[16] Conversely, the firm must disclose the existence of the mineral deposits to the sophisticated investors before it proceeds with its plan to repurchase the stock.[17]

Whether either disclosure rule makes sense or whether there is a sensible way to justify the different duties has long been a source of controversy with respect to commercial transactions, generally, and the trading of securities in particular.[18] But our willingness to expose innocent farmers to the harshness of the market while shielding Wall Street fat cats shows both the range of approaches and an absence of obvious overarching principles.

Other things being equal, disclosure of information is good. One wants the price to reflect underlying values. Only if the information about the underlying value is known can it be incorporated into the market price. Yet the need for disclosure in a liquid market is far less than it appears. Indeed, when the markets are thick enough, information can remain private and still be reflected in the market price. The trading activity of those with knowledge drives the price. It is enough that those with knowledge trade (and are known to trade). In equilibrium, the information that only a few knowledgeable insiders possess becomes embedded (with some noise) in the market price.[19]

Consider the simplest case in which outsiders can observe the trading behavior of someone who is known to possess inside information. Ten individuals are standing in a room and there are ten identical black boxes on a table in the center. The boxes are open and each contains the same unknown amount of cash. One of the individuals is allowed to look inside each of the boxes and count the cash before they are sealed. That person discovers that each box contains $20 but says nothing. After the boxes are sealed, one box is given to each person in the room. Each of the individuals is allowed to keep her box, sell it, or buy boxes from others. No one is permitted to look inside any of the boxes.

The individual who saw what was inside each box quietly approaches different individuals and tries to bargain with them. She tries to sell her own box and offers to buy others. She engages in some trades. Given what she knows, she is, of course, happy to buy any box for less than $20 and sell any box she possesses for more than $20. Those with whom she trades will turn around and trade with others. Those who bargain with the person possessing information will be able to infer something about what she knows, and this information will in turn be reflected in their own trades. As the trading evolves, the price at which everyone else buys or sells converges on $20, even though the only person with knowledge has not said anything about what she saw and would like to keep the information secret.

All that matters is that one individual had access to the information and has an opportunity to trade on the information and that some of the others can observe her trade. As long as the benefits of trade (in this case being able to sell a box for a little bit more than $20 or buy for a little bit less) are greater than the time and energy the informed party spent to learn about the contents of the box, the information will be collected and news of it will spread. There is no need to require the person with inside information to disclose what she saw. Her own trading behavior will soon reveal that to everyone.

When the market is otherwise sufficiently liquid, disclosure requirements are not merely unnecessary but affirmatively harmful. We need to give someone the incentive to look inside the box and put that person in a position to profit when the price rises just above or falls just below $20. Requiring everyone to disclose before trading takes away some of the incentive to spend the time counting the money in the first place.[20] Rules aimed at ensuring transparency can actually create a less efficient market, one that is less liquid and in which prices fail to reflect underlying values.

Returning to the example of the mining company, if the legal regime forced the company to disclose what it knew about the mineral deposits before acquiring the mineral rights, it might never have hired geologists to look for the deposits. The minerals might never have been discovered.

One should not assume, however, that those with private information always drive trade toward the true price. One can imagine an investor who makes a trade with a view to misleading others. To return to the black box hypothetical, the person with knowledge might have a confederate in the room. She sells her box for $15, giving the impression that it is worth no more than this amount. Taking advantage of this misimpression, the confederate buys as many boxes as she can for $15. After everyone is gone, the two meet up and split their windfall between them. (In this case, their profits are the $5 gained on each box purchased, less the $5 lost in creating the false impression that the box contained only $15 rather than $20.)

In addition to the possibility of market manipulations, we need to worry about the way in which dispersed private information can undermine the liquidity of a market. One can imagine environments in which multiple parties possess private information, but none of them has an incentive to disclose what they know, even though each would be better off if everyone disclosed what they knew.

Consider a variation on the ten black boxes. The original owner of the black boxes puts cash in each of the black boxes on five different occasions, but only one of the individuals is present on each occasion. Each person knows only the amount of cash added when she was present. The ten individuals know that one of them was present on each of the five occasions but cannot distinguish those who have some knowledge from those who are completely ignorant. Each of the ten is again given a box.

Those who saw some money being added to the box have no incentive to reveal it. Revealing information helps others ascertain the value of the box but does not help them. Collectively the individuals in the room possess all the information necessary to ascertain the amount of cash in each of the black boxes, but no single individual has an incentive to disclose what she knows. If all were forced to disclose what they knew, everyone would know the value of each box and all would be better off, but no one has an incentive to do this on her own.

We face a collective action problem in which the individual benefits of disclosure are small, but the benefits of disclosure to the group are large. The contrast between this example and the first illustrates the trade-off between discouraging those with information from trading on it and ensuring that the market is sufficiently transparent that people will be willing to trade. Existing theories of market design do not offer many lessons about the liquidity/transparency trade-off.[21]

Misrepresentations

Even after we settle on how much needs to be disclosed in any context, we still need a way to understand what counts as a misrepresentation. Misrepresentations include not only outright lying but also behavior and actions that are misleading. In some environments, an answer that is technically speaking completely accurate may nevertheless constitute a misrepresentation.

Consider the apocryphal advertising slogan promoting tuna in the face of strong demand for salmon, "Guaranteed not to turn pink in the can." This is a misrepresentation to the extent it would lead a reasonable person to believe that salmon turns pink only after it is canned. Another example can be found in the too old vaudeville joke in which the man walking a cute dog is asked whether his dog bites. When the man replies that he does not, the stranger reaches down to pet the dog and has a piece of his hand bitten off. Screaming in pain, the stranger says, "You said your dog doesn't bite!" The man replies, "That is true, but this isn't my dog."

The most common misrepresentation case arises when someone says something that, while true on its own terms, is misleading in light of what has come before. In the words of *Restatement of Torts,* one is required to disclose "matters known to him that he knows to be necessary to prevent his partial or ambiguous statement of the facts from being misleading."[22] One is also required to disclose "subsequently acquired information that he knows will make untrue or misleading a previous representation that when made was true or believed to be so."

Some jurisdictions in recent years have also required disclosure when one party to the transaction knows that disclosure "would correct a mistake of the other party as to a basic assumption on which that party is making the contract and if nondisclosure of the fact amounts to a failure to act in good faith and in accordance with reasonable standards of fair dealing."[23] The owner of a building brings in a second contractor to repair the mistakes of a previous one and fails to disclose a number of defects that are not readily observable that will make the job much more costly than first appears.[24] I have a storeroom by the ocean that I have converted to an amusement center containing a number of different concessions with pinball machines and other devices that might or might not be legal. I sell my amusement center to you knowing that the police plan to raid the establishment and close down many parts of it.[25] I own a rubbish collection business and sell it to you knowing that there is a strong possibility that the city will let a contract for the rubbish collection and render the business superfluous.[26] Courts have not decided these cases uniformly, but the difficulties they raise in identifying what counts as a misrepresentation complicate the blackletter doctrine of *Laidlaw* considerably.[27]

Justice Marshall found that Organ's evasiveness prevented him from finding in Organ's favor. A jury needed to hear the case and decide whether Organ's actions when asked whether he had news that would affect the price were, in the words of Laidlaw's lawyer, "equivalent to a false answer, and as much calculated to deceive as the communication of the most fabulous intelligence."[28]

Laidlaw contains one additional complication that Marshall neglects. Marshall asserts that Laidlaw took advantage of information "equally accessible" to both parties. This turns out not to be true.[29] Organ learned that the war was over before anyone else, not because of special diligence on his part but through the brother of his business partner, who was the aide-de-camp to the commander of naval defenses in New Orleans. The brother had been among those whom Jackson sent to negotiate the exchange of prisoners and the return of escaped slaves. He learned that the treaty had been signed and that the war was over from the British, and he sought to profit from it on his return. He conveyed this information to his brother, who then tried to make money for them both. Far from acquiring "equally accessible" information through careful diligence, Organ acquired knowledge of the war's end through his private contacts with government officials.

At this time, the brother might not have been under any legal duty to refrain from trading on information he learned as a result of government service, but such a legal duty seems desirable. Those who create a market cannot expect people to come and trade on it if they allow themselves to profit from what they learn in the course of running it. The government stands in essentially the same position, especially in New Orleans during the War of 1812, where martial law was in place.

Disclosure and Relationships of Trust

How much you have to disclose is going to turn on who you are and the person with whom you are dealing. In many academic debates, people simply speak past each other. The paradigm for one is two merchants in a Turkish bazaar, and the paradigm for the other is a fast-talking salesman and an innocent consumer. Rarely is an effort made to reconcile the two different ways of looking at the world. Much ultimately turns on how important you think it is that people are able to exploit the information they have. How much does the information represent an investment? How often do such investments bring about transactions that are desirable?

Moreover, the relationship itself changes the inferences one is inclined to draw about the background facts. If one diamond merchant buys a stone from another that each can inspect, there is much less likelihood of misrepresentation than if a jeweler buys the same stone from a widow. When two diamond merchants interact, they each possess identical expertise. They rely on their own knowledge and have less need to ask their trading partners for information or to expect them to provide it. When a widow approaches a jeweler, she often looks to the jeweler for information about the stone. She is more likely to ask questions, and there is more room for the jeweler's answers (or nonanswers) to be evasive or misleading. An observation that might be clear to a fellow merchant may not be clear to a consumer.

In some cases, the law may go beyond simply drawing additional inferences from the surrounding facts. A duty to disclose may arise by virtue of the relationship that exists between two parties. One of the perennial debates in the law revolves around the relative importance of status and contract. If our notions of commerce center around corporations engaged in Darwinian struggles, clear ground rules may be all that matters. But if we view the world as a network of relationships, we may pay attention to them and their dynamics and adjust responsibilities accordingly. In such a world, we require little of a merchant when dealing with another, but we do require a jeweler who buys a stone from a widow to be forthcoming. We want contract law to impose responsibilities on the more sophisticated party.

Postcontractual Disclosure

Once two merchants enter into a contract with each other, their duty of good faith toward one another takes on a different character. Even if one accepts the notion that merchants need to do little more than be affirmatively honest while they are negotiating a deal, once they have entered into a contract, the standards to which they are held may be higher.

Richard Posner explored this issue in *Market Street Associates Ltd. Partnership v. Frey.*[30]

In 1968, a retail chain entered into a sale and leaseback arrangement with General Electric Pension Trust in order to finance its growth. Under the arrangement, the chain sold properties to General Electric, and GE leased them back for a term of twenty-five years. A clause buried in the middle of the lease entitled the chain to request that GE finance the costs and expenses of construction of additional improvements. Both were required to negotiate in good faith, but if the negotiations failed, the chain was entitled to repurchase the property at a price roughly equal to the price at which it sold the property to GE in the first place, plus 6 percent a year for each year since the original purchase. If the average annual appreciation in the property exceeded this amount and GE failed to agree to the financing, the chain would be able to buy back the property for less than its market value.

Two decades later, a successor to the retail chain, Market Street, sought to make major improvements to it. Market Street asked GE to finance improvements to the property. GE refused, largely on the ground that it did not make any investments of less than $7 million.

At this point, Market Street invoked the clause entitling it to terminate the lease and repurchase the property for the prescribed amount. GE refused to turn the property over. It asserted that, in failing to point out that its refusal to finance the improvements would trigger the option to terminate, Market Street had failed to act in good faith. The trial court found in favor of GE on the ground that Market Street should have advised GE that it was requesting financing pursuant to the clause that triggered the right to repurchase. Market Street had a duty to ensure that GE was aware of a clause that would effectively penalize it if it refused to negotiate. It could not take advantage of a clause that was drafted long before, indeed so long before that those now acting on behalf of GE were likely working for someone else at the time of the original deal or too young to be working at all.

Market Street appealed and the case came before Richard Posner. For Posner, Market Street was not obliged to remind its contracting opposite to read its own contracts. As he put it, "it would be quixotic as well as presumptuous for judges to undertake through contract law to raise the ethical standards of the nation's business people." But this did not mean that Market Street was off the hook.

The contract itself did not spell out what disclosure duties each party had, so contract law needed to fill in the gaps. It did this by requiring parties to act in "good faith." It was the responsibility of the judge to figure out what this meant. As Posner saw it, "To be able to correct your partner's mistake at zero cost to yourself, and decide not to do so, is a species of opportunistic behavior that the parties would have expressly forbidden in the contract had they foreseen it." It was not permissible for one to

> take deliberate advantage of an oversight by your contract partner concerning his rights under the contract. Such taking advantage is not the exploitation of superior knowledge or the avoidance of unbargained-for expense; it is sharp dealing. Like theft, it has no social product, and also like theft it induces costly defensive expenditures, in the form of overelaborate disclaimers or investigations into the trustworthiness of a prospective contract partner, just as the prospect of theft induces expenditures on locks.

Posner found the outcome of the case unclear on the basis of the record before him. It was possible that GE deserved what it got for failing to read its own lease. For Posner, the dispositive question was whether Market Street Associates "tried to trick" GE and succeeded in doing so.

But once one reduces the problem to one of filling in the gaps in the written contract, why should one think that the duty that advanced the mutual interests of the parties would be an obligation not to trick the other party?[31] Why should this point demarcate the limit of what parties would want if they could bargain over the question explicitly? Why would not parties want disclosure of information whenever conveying the information was both easy and important? When two parties enter into a contractual relationship, why would they impose on each other obligations to review every word of the documents to every deal each time they interacted?

But, by the same logic, one can also fault Posner for doing too much. GE was far from a babe in the woods. If GE was too foolish to read its own contracts, why should those contracting with it be obliged to refrain from taking advantage of its stupidity? Before parties enter a contract, there is no obligation to tell the other how to negotiate a better deal. Why exactly should this change once the contract is entered? It may not make sense for Posner to turn over the matter to a trial judge and jury and have them assess whether what Market Street did amounted to trickery.

Posner asserts that a test focused on deliberate advantage taking would make both parties to a contract better off. They would want such an arrangement because it is in their mutual interest to maximize the benefits from trade. This is completely correct in theory, but it works in practice only if the fact finder will do a good job of ascertaining what each party knew and what each was obliged to tell the other. GE and Marketplace may be willing to tolerate the potential for advantage taking by the other. It may reduce the risk that a court will later find that one or the other did too little hand-holding of the other during the subsequent negotiations, hand-holding that is neither cheap nor in either's self-interest.

Posner uses the familiar heuristic of speculating about the hypothetical bargain that the parties would strike between themselves. The exercise is not about substantive terms of the contract but rather about the ground rules that govern the subsequent interaction between them. There seem to be two forces at work that pull in opposite directions. Merchants want to limit advantage taking, but they also want to limit the ability of the courts to rewrite their bargains.

When left to their own devices, sophisticated business people often waive protections that courts offer them. One example is a custom that has emerged among sophisticated vulture investors. They commonly trade with each other while possessing material information unknown to the other and to the public at large. To avoid the disclosure rules that the law might impose, they exchange what are called "Big Boy" letters. Each party asserts that it is a sophisticated investor (a "Big Boy"), recognizes that the other may possess material, nonpublic information, and affirms that it is not in any way relying on the other's failure to disclose that information. Whether Big Boy letters work remains to be seen,[32] but they do at least seem to reflect that sophisticated parties would rather do without the laws designed to protect them.[33] They want to live in a world in which everyone is constantly on guard.

Vulture investors are crucially different from General Electric and Market Street and many other commercial parties over several dimensions. Vulture investors work in small firms and spend their time monitoring a relatively small number of discrete positions over comparatively short periods of time. Many commercial actors, by contrast, are corporate entities. They enter complicated relationships that last years and, as in *Market Street*, sometimes decades. The relationship may be defined through many different documents, each running hundreds of pages. Those doing the negotiating turn over continuously during the course of the relationship.

In such an environment, one should expect conventions to emerge that reflect these realities. When no single individual knows the details of the entire transaction, it may be in the interests of all the parties to be spared the costs of relearning the entire history of the relationship each time they interact with one other.

Before word processors allowed different documents to be compared electronically, lawyers adopted the practice of relying on their opposites to redline documents to show changes between drafts. Failure to mark a change in a document, no matter how trivial, was a hanging crime. Parties would walk away from deals if they discovered a change that had been left unmarked. Such a discovery was a clock that struck thirteen. They had no way to know how much else was not right. The risk that a court would subsequently hold them liable to a contract term of which they were unaware was too great. Parties in a relationship such as the one that GE and Market Street had might have a similar custom. Disclosure norms might emerge in such environments.

For all the reasons we have discussed, it would be a mistake to assume that such background conventions themselves should be identical with the legal rule that binds the parties and defines what constitutes good faith. Nevertheless, it would be useful to find out what these conventions are. If those who took an action that would have the effect of terminating or profoundly altering the relationship routinely flag this fact even when they would rather not, then the actions in *Market Street* look much more like sharp practice than if such notice were never provided. Similarly, if there were a strong norm that each party was on its own every time the other side proposed some course that affected their bargain, one might take a different approach to defining "good faith." Even if the legal realists went too far in thinking that the law can take its cues from mercantile norms, they may still provide a tool to get one's bearings.

6

Mistake, Excuse, and Implicit Terms

Mistake

In the course of the contractual relationship, many kinds of "mistakes" are possible. We have already encountered one type. I promise to sell cotton on the *Peerless,* and you promise to buy cotton on the *Peerless.* I mean the December *Peerless* and you mean the October *Peerless.* We have each made a mistake about what the other is thinking. Is there a meeting of the minds sufficient to form a contract, and if so, on what terms? But there are other types of mistakes as well.

We might have a scrivener's error. We both agree that I will sell you a hundred widgets, but the written document says 1,000. Should the writing trump the actual agreement of the parties? The answer is "no" in many cases. One party can bring an action to "reform" the contract. Such actions make eminent sense, provided, of course, that courts do a good job of identifying these sorts of errors.

The doctrine of "mutual mistake" involves yet another type of error. We are on the same wavelength, but we are on the wrong wavelength. I promise to sell you something and you promise to buy it, but we both turn out to be mistaken with respect to a critical attribute of the thing being sold. We have a perfect meeting of the minds, but the state of the world is not what either of us thought it was. Is it so far from what we thought that the deal should be called off?

Sherwood v. Walker is the canonical case that raises this issue. T.C. Sherwood was a banker interested in buying a cow. Hiram Walker told him that he had a few head on his Greenfield farm. Sherwood could go out and look at them, but they "were probably barren." Sherwood did in fact go out to the farm and offered to buy Rose the Second of Aberlone.

The purchase price was five and a half cents a pound, less fifty pounds shrinkage, a price term used for cattle bound for slaughter. There is no suggestion, however, that either party thought Sherwood would slaughter the cow.

After the contract was signed but before Sherwood picked up the cow, Walker discovered that Rose was pregnant and refused to turn her over. Walker, of course, could not call off the contract if he were the only one who was mistaken. As we saw in our discussion of *Laidlaw,* Sherwood is entitled to profit from his diligence. It is no fun to walk through back pastures to see if any of the cows the owner thinks are barren are in fact pregnant. If the legal rule required Sherwood to disclose to Walker that Walker's own cow was pregnant, he may not bother trudging through the pasture the next time around. Hiram Walker will be sitting at his dinner table drinking cheap whiskey and eating steak.

Walker justified his refusal to deliver Rose on the ground that both parties were fundamentally mistaken as to the true nature of the cow. Because of this mutual mistake, the contract should be voided.

Mutual mistake is an elusive concept. To make sense of it, we need to understand how the facts of *Sherwood* are any different from the ordinary case in which I buy a share of stock in a firm shortly before it discovers a new gold mine. Those who trade seek to buy low and sell high. They expect to keep their profits when they do, and the law generally lets them.

Nothing is ever known with certainty. Walker had told Sherwood that the cow was "probably" barren. Sherwood did not intend to butcher the cow and thought that perhaps it would breed. He was taking a chance. Everything is a gamble. Sherwood won the gamble. Low-probability events sometimes come to pass, and they cut both ways. The goose may lay golden eggs. The racehorse you buy from me can drop dead tomorrow.

A mutual mistake case is the flip side of a warranty case. Warranties matter when we both think the goods I am selling you are fine, but they are not.[1] In the case of mutual mistake, we both think that the thing is bad, when it turns out to be good. This problem is yet another variation of the more general problem of filling in gaps in a contract that is necessarily incomplete.

Other things being equal, it may make sense to let the gains (and losses) lie where they fall. But just as we have reasons for imposing duties on the seller when the goods are worse than either expects, there are reasons to undo the transaction when things prove more favorable. One rationale for mutual mistake focuses on the comparative competences of the parties after the mistake is uncovered. I am a breeder and you are a butcher. We think the cow is barren, and you buy it from me for five cents a pound, plus fifty pounds shrinkage. It turns out to be fertile. This transaction no longer makes sense. The seller may be the person better equipped to take care of a fertile cow. After all, what are you, a butcher, going to do with a pregnant cow? Allowing the transaction to go forward merely puts you in a position where you have a cow you need to resell, perhaps back to me.

I find an old table that has been in my family forever. I decide to use it as a workbench in my garage, but first I want to have it refinished. You are a furniture refinisher specializing in workbenches. You agree to refinish it for $100, the going rate for refinishing workbenches. As you start your work, you discover that it is a priceless Chippendale dining room table easily worth $1 million. Refinishing a Chippendale, however, is a completely different enterprise from stripping varnish off a junk shop table. A contract concerning the former is something altogether different from one concerning the latter. Are you liable for the cost of refinishing a Chippendale, a job that costs tens of thousands? Are you free to treat it as if it were an ordinary junk-shop table and apply an industrial-strength polyurethane coating to it? Neither outcome makes sense. The sensible outcome is that we cancel the contract.

Of course, not any mistake should be sufficient. In transactions of any complexity, it is rare that everything turns out as planned. Issues nearly always arise that neither party expected. If the parties had known about them ahead of time, one or the other would have asked for more time or some other change in the contract. But these sorts of mutual mistakes do not alter the fundamental relationship between the parties. Even had the parties known about the complications, they would still have entered into a contract with one another. The basic contours of the contract would have been the same. But in the case of the old table from my attic, the mistake goes to the heart of the deal. The job requires expertise and tools of an altogether different kind. Indeed, things depart so much from what either of us expected that, had we known the true state of affairs, we would never have dealt with each other in the first place on any terms.

The person who restores workbenches lacks the expertise to restore priceless antiques. This case differs from the one that arises when the mutual mistake concerns a matter that leaves unaltered the rationale that brought the parties together in the first instance. You are an expert in restoring Chippendale tables, and you agree to restore my Chippendale table for a fixed price. Restoring the table proves more expensive and difficult than you expected. Mutual mistake should not apply here. As the person with the expertise in restoring tables, this is exactly the type of risk you assumed when you entered into the contract with me to do the restoration for a fixed price.

Mutual mistake has at least one additional virtue.[2] It makes the problem of distinguishing between silence and misrepresentations marginally easier. Some who read *Sherwood v. Walker* have the suspicion that Sherwood may have known that the cow was pregnant at the time he bought it. Let us assume this state of affairs. Sherwood really knew what was going on and did nothing to inform Walker. It was not a mutual mistake at all. Only Walker was mistaken.

This alone should not lead us to unwind the transaction. As Justice Marshall told us in *Laidlaw,* Sherwood is under no obligation to disclose the information. But it is a problem if Sherwood learned that Rose was pregnant and then misled Walker. If Walker had asked Sherwood whether his inspection revealed anything about the cow, Sherwood had to disclose it. If Sherwood made any remarks about the condition of the cow after he discovered it was pregnant, they had to be truthful. Moreover, if Sherwood had previously inspected the cow and told Walker he thought the cow was barren, the law of misrepresentation requires Sherwood to reveal what he discovered now that he knows what he said before is not true. In short, if Sherwood learns the cow is pregnant, he has to walk a very narrow line in his later interactions with Walker. The doctrine of mutual mistake makes it easy to tell whether he has done this.

With the doctrine of mutual mistake, Sherwood can get the benefit of his bargain only by revealing that he had knowledge. Only by asserting that he had learned the cow was fertile can he keep the doctrine of mutual mistake from operating. Forcing him to reveal what he learned and when he learned it makes it easier to tell whether anything he said later was a misrepresentation. There is a clear benchmark against which to assess his subsequent statements. Sherwood will be rewarded for special knowledge only if he did not engage in any sharp practice.

Restatement (Second) of Contracts §152 establishes three requirements for avoidance on grounds of mutual mistake. The party adversely affected must show:

1. The mistake goes to a basic assumption on which the contract was made;
2. The mistake has a material effect on the agreed exchange of performances; and
3. The mistake is not one of which he bears the risk.

This multipart test may be just a fancy way of asking what the fully dickered bargain would have looked like. Trade usage may be the best way of getting at this. The responsibilities of the seller and the buyer may change across industries. The responsibilities of the seller of a bull may be different from the seller of a cow. The responsibilities of sellers of calves may be different from the sellers of cattle that are fully grown.

Repose

Sherwood brought a replevin action. Instead of seeking damages, he demanded that Walker turn over the cow. Under the law as it existed at the time, once the goods were specifically identified to the contract and in a deliverable state, title to them passed. Hence, in the absence of mutual mistake, the law would treat Sherwood as the owner of Rose the Second of Aberlone. There is nothing in *Sherwood v. Walker* that suggests that the case would have come out differently if the cow had already been delivered and Walker was suing Sherwood.

Nevertheless, courts are less inclined to unwind transactions as time passes. If Sherwood had kept this cow for several years and Rose only then produced a calf, we might have a quite different case. It would be much harder to unscramble things. For example, it would seem that Walker should have to compensate Sherwood for the costs of taking care of the cow. Moreover, Sherwood may have incurred expenses, such as hiring new staff, under the assumption that he would have an extra cow. He might argue that he is entitled to be reimbursed for these costs.

Quite apart from how any of these expenses are calculated, we also need to bear in mind the shadow that such a doctrine casts. To the extent that a legal doctrine allows a transaction to be undone, buyers can never be sure that they can keep what they have acquired. Contract rights themselves are layered on top of property rights. We want to facilitate trade so people can acquire assets and use them productively. I want to acquire Blackacre, build a factory on it, and employ thousands of workers. The greater the risk that you can reappear at some future time and demand Blackacre back, the less inclined I shall be to make the investment doing all this requires. Property rights are secure only to the extent that completed transactions cannot be undone.

The law cares about repose. Recall *Citizen Kane*. Charles Foster Kane grew up rich because one day his mother, an impoverished innkeeper, got a deed from a boarder who could not pay what he owed. The deed turned out to be for land that contained the Colorado lode. No one suggests that the boarder can reappear and take back the land.

The threshold for what counts as a mistake sufficient to unsettle the transaction may change by virtue of the relationship between the parties. *Jackson v. Seymour* provides an illustration.[3] In February 1947, Lucy Jackson sold her brother, Benjamin Seymour, thirty-one acres of land for $275. He told her what he believed—that it was land suitable only for pasture and that $275 was a good price for it. After buying it, Seymour discovered that, unbeknownst to either his sister or him, the land contained valuable timber. He proceeded to sell it for ten times what he paid for the property. When the sister found out, she sued and demanded that he disgorge his profits.

The problem is again one of mutual mistake. Neither one knew the value of the land. Given the passage of time, a court would not unravel the transaction if it had been between two merchants at arm's length. Nevertheless, Jackson, by virtue of the trust she reposed in her brother, may be entitled to undo transactions in a way that she would not had she been dealing with a complete stranger.

At the same time that the law is more reluctant to unwind transactions if enough time passes, it gives more scope to a mistake when transactions can be unraveled quickly and at little cost. I go in to a store and see a rookie Roger Maris baseball card for $1. The owner knows the value of the card, but her clerk does not and he misfiles it. The clerk is the only person in the store when I come to buy it. It is not a mutual mistake. I possess the valuable information and am under no duty to disclose it. Nevertheless, *Laidlaw* might not apply if the owner discovers the mistake quickly enough after the sale.[4]

When there is something that is clearly wrong and the other party knows it, there may be little sense in allowing the transaction to go forward. It is like the doctrine of last-clear chance, which in tort law relieves someone of the consequences of negligent action because the other party had a subsequent opportunity to avoid the accident at little cost.

Consider another case. You are a general contractor who makes a bid to build a school but slip a digit and make a bid that is too low.[5] You are awarded the contract by virtue of your low bid, but the next day, before there is any reliance, you discover your mistake. You attempt to call off the deal. This case could be like the baseball card case. The mistake might be so large that, with the other bids in hand, the owner knew or should have known that something was amiss.

Courts may grant relief for unilateral mistake even when the other party was not aware of it. What matters is that the costs of unwinding the transaction are low enough. If the mistake is discovered very quickly and there has been no reliance, allowing the owner to enforce this contract against the general contractor vindicates no social policy, beyond inducing people who prepare bids to be more careful. Investing in such care is a good idea, but like anything else, it can be overdone. For her part, the owner who is getting a good deal has done nothing particularly praiseworthy. She is not exercising great judgment nor being especially savvy. If we enforce this contract, in the absence of reliance, the owner is just lucky. One party gets rich and the other gets poor.

There is also a downside to enforcing contracts in the case of mistake that we should recognize as well. The contractor who wins the bid as a result of the mistake may be the wrong person for the job. The person who would have otherwise had the winning bid might have been able to build the school more cheaply or more quickly. Holding the general contractor who makes a mistake to the deal leads to waste. This danger may outweigh the way such a rule reduces the incentive of contractors to check their figures carefully before they submit their bids.

We can recall at this point our discussion of expectation damages. Some of the reluctance to embrace expectation damages stems from the way the measure operates in the case of a breach that occurs just after parties enter into the contract. If expectation damages were denied in the case of a quick breach, there is no need for a separate doctrine to handle the problem of the contractor who makes a mistaken bid. There would be a breach but no damages.

Excuse

Another species of mistake falls under the umbrella of "excuse." Mutual mistake involves a misapprehension about the present state of the world. Neither of us thought the cow was pregnant. Excuse involves a failure to account for a future event. Neither of us expected the fire that burned down the stable and killed the cow.

The core excuse case involves casualty to identified goods. We touched on this doctrine briefly in our discussion of *Raffles*. I promise to sell you my red Porsche. Just before I turn it over to you, it is struck by lightning and disintegrates. You sue me. You claim that I broke my promise to sell you my Porsche. I reply that the law should not force me to keep a promise that, by its nature, cannot be kept. The car I promised to sell you does not exist anymore.

A legal rule that refuses to call off my obligation does not demand the impossible. To be sure, the car no longer exists, but I can still pay damages. From a Holmesian perspective, my ability to perform is not relevant. I simply have to pay you damages if the promised event (my delivery of the Porsche) does not come to pass for whatever reason.

The rationale for releasing me from my obligation turns not on impossibility but on a sensible understanding of our implicit bargain. Neither one of us ever thought that lightning would strike the car. But we share an intuition about what we would have done if we had thought about it. We would have provided that the deal was conditioned on my car still being around at the time that the risk of loss was to shift from me to you. When there is casualty to identified goods before risk of loss shifts, the deal should be called off.

But the intuition we have about a one-shot sale of a used car between amateurs may not translate well to other contexts. In the hypothetical involving the lightning striking the Porsche, the stakes were low. Even if I were held to my promise, I would owe no damages. In all likelihood, I agreed to sell you the Porsche at the market price and you incurred no out-of-pocket costs. Relax either of these assumptions, and the intuition that excuse is a sensible doctrine is harder to make.

Consider the effects that excuse doctrine has when expectation damages prove substantial. If there were no excuse doctrine and the value of the Porsche rose sharply before delivery, I would be required to make you whole for the difference between the value of the Porsche and what you promised to pay for it. For this reason, I would invest in care to the extent of the full market value of the car. This changes in the presence of excuse.

Assume I sold you the car for $10,000 for delivery in a month's time. In the interim, its value rose to $20,000. In the absence of excuse doctrine, I would change my insurance to reflect the increase in value and increase the resources I spend in taking care of it commensurately. But when excuse doctrine exists, I have only $10,000 worth of insurance and take care as if it were worth only that amount. You must insure the increment and try to persuade me to take extra care.

Of course, we could reach a deal with each other. If it were sensible to invest in additional care because of the increase in value of the Porsche, you would persuade me to do it if bargaining costs were low enough. Other things being equal, however, the legal rule should not require this extra bargaining. This is the point of having expectation damages.

It would seem that the law should give one or the other of us the incentive to take whatever steps to protect the car that were prudent. While the car is in my possession and under my care, that person would seem to be me. The law should ensure that I bear the entire loss. The excuse doctrine, however, keeps this from happening. In short, the excuse doctrine seems largely irrelevant when there are no damages, and when it does matter, it introduces the wrong set of incentives.

This aspect of excuse may well be one that matters more inside the law school classroom than outside it. In most of the cases involving excuse, the problems arise not because of changes in market value but rather because of the resources that one or more of the parties has invested in the contract. The challenge is one of finding a way to unravel the transaction sensibly.

Taylor v. Caldwell is the old chestnut. A theater burned down, and the person who had been promised the use of the space sued. Expectation damages should not be large in such a case. There is a duty to mitigate. If Taylor could hire another theater and get the same profits, there would be no damages. If the show were so unusual that it could be mounted only in this particular theater, there would be lost profits in theory, but a court would likely find these too speculative. For these reasons, those in the position of Taylor usually are seeking to recover the expenses incurred in preparing for a performance that can no longer take place.

Opera Co. of Boston v. Wolf Trap illustrates the difficulties we face.[6] The performance of an opera had to be called off because an electrical storm knocked out the power before a performance. The opera company was ready and willing to perform, but it could not perform without electricity. Electricity was needed both for the stage and to ensure that the audience could find their way from their cars. The dispute is not over the profits that might have been made if the performance had taken place but rather over the expenses incurred to mount the show. Someone has to bear them.

We should not conclude too quickly that losses should be shared on the ground it was really no one's fault. Even if it is no one's fault, incentives matter. Excuse might take away the incentive from people like Wolf Trap to install backup generators or buy insurance. Those who run Wolf Trap may not have good knowledge about the likelihood of a power failure or steps needed to prevent it, but they have a much better idea than a touring opera company.

We also need to put the problem in the larger perspective before we can be confident that excusing parties from their obligations makes sense. Remember that Wolf Trap and the opera company are not the only two parties who are affected by all of this. Do not forget the opera singers. Let us assume that the opera to be performed was *Aida*. The tenor is sitting there in the dark wearing a cumbersome pseudo-Egyptian costume. He is sweating, and the heavy makeup is dripping. He is there only because the opera company promised to pay him $10,000.

If Wolf Trap's obligations to Opera Company of Boston are excused, what about Opera Company's obligations to the tenor? If the power failure is no one's fault, why should not Opera Company be released from its obligations to the tenor? An experience at the opera in my mother's youth shows that the problem does not stop here.

It is Saturday afternoon, February 26, 1938. Everyone is excited. Zinka Milanov, the renown Croatian-born soprano, is Aida. Bruna Castalagna is Amneris. And Giovanni Martinelli, the great Italian tenor of the age, is Radames. My mother saved her allowance for months to hear this *Aida* at the Metropolitan Opera. The curtain rises, and Giovanni Martinelli is about to sing "Celeste Aida." He appears on stage, and as he stands under the hot stage lights, it becomes clear that he has one of the worst hangovers you can imagine or, as the official version later went, an acute case of indigestion. A few bars into "Celeste Aida," he faints. This is completely unexpected. No one had ever done this before.[7]

You cannot have an *Aida* without a Radames, but whatever its legal rights, the Met did not try to argue that it was released from its promise to mount the show. My mother never had to confront the doctrine of excuse in her youth. The curtain comes down, there is a twenty-minute delay, and then the curtain opens again. Dressed in Martinelli's costume is Frederick Jagel. Even though it had never happened before, the Met had a backup tenor on call, just in case. Bruna Castalagna taps her foot on the floor, looks at the conductor, and says, "Commence," and everyone is off to the races. They skip "Celeste Aida," but you cannot have everything.

As between members of the audience and an opera company, it would seem that the opera company should suffer the consequences if the tenor is indisposed. It should not matter how unexpected the risk is. The opera company is the superior risk bearer. Legal rules may not play a large role, given all the other forces at work, but they should at least push the parties in the right direction. It should, at the margin, lead the Met to ask whether to have a backup tenor because of the risk that Giovanni Martinelli might be hung over. It may not make sense to have a backup in a smaller town with fewer tenors wandering around, but it still makes sense for the opera company to have an incentive to ensure its singers stay sober.

In *Wolf Trap*, the case was remanded to the district court with a general, and not very useful, three-part test. A party is excused when

1. There is an unexpected occurrence of an intervening act;
2. Such occurrence was of such a character that its nonoccurrence was a basic assumption of the agreement of the parties; and
3. That occurrence made performance impracticable.[8]

At first blush, the doctrine of excuse is going to be widely available in cases like *Wolf Trap*. The failure of electricity was unexpected, having electricity was something everyone assumed would be available, and without electricity we cannot have a show. But we put a gloss on the word "unexpected." The intervening event has to be one for which the relevant party has not assumed the responsibility. The court in the *Wolf Trap* case seems to understand part of the need to unpack the idea of what kinds of "unexpected" events let Wolf Trap off the hook by focusing on the idea of foreseeability. The court talks about whether the loss of electricity was "of such reasonable likelihood that the obligor should not merely foresee the risk but, because of the degree of its likelihood, the obligor should have guarded against it."[9] But why should the obligation to guard against a risk turn on its degree of likelihood? Why should losses be shared as the event becomes less probable? The Met is still better able than my mother to find backup tenors, even if tenors rarely fall ill in the middle of a performance. Probability alone does not seem the touchstone. What matters is the ability to guard against the event, regardless of how probable it is. When the insurance company insures your house, neither one of you expects the house to burn down, but the insurance company has assumed the risk of this low-probability event.

The problem becomes harder to the extent that money has changed hands. Let us assume that the contract required Opera Company to pay Wolf Trap $100,000 one week before the performance for the use of the facility. Can Opera Company insist on the return of the money if performance is excused? The early English cases suggest that Opera Company could not. Indeed, they held that if those in the position of Opera Company had not already paid the money they were contractually obliged to pay, they could be forced to do so.[10] The effect of this rule was to freeze the position of the parties at where they had agreed to be at the moment that the unexpected event came along.

Some have defended the original English rule on the ground that parties usually organize their affairs in such a way that the ledgers between the parties are always in rough equipoise.[11] Wolf Trap can insist on a large deposit in those cases in which it has large expenditures. This rule is, of course, not completely satisfactory. Under such a rule, my mother would have no legal right even to get her money back when Giovanni Martinelli keeled over. At the time of the unexpected event, she had already paid for her ticket.

Some have advocated unwinding the transaction to the extent that one side has provided a benefit to the other. But we cannot easily implement a rule that entitles the parties to recover for any benefit they have conferred on the other. Recall the facts of the *Fibrosa* case.[12] A Polish firm orders a custom piece of equipment from a British firm in 1938. It pays £1,000 in advance. The British firm starts designing it. War comes along. When it is over, the Polish firm has no need for the machine. It argues that allowing the manufacturer to keep the money would unjustly enrich it. The court held that the Polish firm could recover its deposit. But this outcome does not account for the expenses that the British firm incurred. Later legislation gave the court discretion to allow a deduction for expenses incurred before the intervening event if it "considers it just to do so."[13]

But even apart from these difficulties of recovering money already paid, it is hard to know what to count in figuring out the benefits one party bestows on another. The facts of *Carroll v. Bowersock* illustrate.[14] A building was destroyed by fire while undergoing renovation. The court found that the fire excused the owner from its obligation to the builder doing the renovations, but the builder had already removed the old floor and installed concrete footings. The court found that this work constituted a benefit to the owner, even though the fire took the value of this work away. In another case, a contractor had done samples, shop drawings, and tests before the state canceled the prime contract. Excuse applied, but the contractor got back for its expenses.[15] The work that had been done, even if not incorporated into the structure, was still of value to the other party.

If we apply this logic to the tenor, it would seem he should be able to recover money spent traveling to Wolf Trap and staying in hotels. The time he has spent rehearsing seems a benefit to Opera Company. He now has to get his costume cleaned. None of this seems different from shop drawings or other preparatory work.

Once we start in this direction, we quickly have a rule that is aimed at both restoring the status quo ante and then granting recovery for reliance expenditures. The tenor should not enjoy the benefit of his bargain, but he should not have to suffer by virtue of the power failure. But once one gets on this train, it is hard to get off. By virtue of singing in *Aida* at Wolf Trap, the tenor gives up the chance in Cleveland for the same fee. His reliance damages are in fact $10,000. In the counterfactual world in which he had never entered into the contract with Opera Company, he would have made $10,000 singing Radames someplace else.

But even if we do not go this far, we still need a way to cabin damage recoveries. One possibility is to put the responsibility for expenses incurred on the party best able to prevent the damage. Wolf Trap takes the fall vis-à-vis Opera Company. It has the burden of either getting a backup generator or buying insurance from Lloyds against the contingency that the electricity will fail. And Opera Company takes the fall vis-à-vis the tenor, which it can cover because of what it gets from Wolf Trap.

We can allow limited damage awards based on notions of relative blameworthiness. Opera Company gets reliance expenditures back from Wolf Trap, and the tenor gets reliance expenditures back from Opera Company. This rule may seem the fairest, but in a world in which reliance is a good proxy for expectation, we are now back to a rule that is close to one that does not allow excuse at all. Wolf Trap broke its contract with Opera Company, Opera Company broke its contract with the tenor, and both must pay damages.

Another possibility is to have something like a negligence rule. Wolf Trap is let off the hook only in those cases in which the electricity would have failed regardless of any steps it took. The Met has to have a backup tenor, but the opera company in Arkansas does not. If you have behaved reasonably, we call off the expectation damages rule. Providing you can measure all of this well enough, you still get the right set of incentives.

To one degree or another, these approaches seem to reflect that an underlying impulse is to prevent innocent parties from incurring a burden they do not deserve. But when something truly unexpected happens and everyone is innocent, this is inevitable. Someone will have to take the fall. What we cannot have is a rule that gives a genuine reliance recovery to all who were not at fault. This is a rule that allows everyone to win, and that just is not possible.

If the tenor recovers reliance damages from Opera Company, there is no logical reason why the equally innocent Opera Company should not recover reliance damages from him. While the tenor has spent money getting to Wolf Trap, Opera Company has spent a lot of money on sets and costumes. If Opera Company has to pay the tenor for his plane ticket, it would seem that the tenor should have to pay for money spent on the elephants.

Before you talk about why it is unfair to hold the tenor or Opera Company or Wolf Trap liable for something that was not its fault, remember that you cannot have a rule that provides that innocent parties can recover their losses when there is an unforeseeable event for which no one is responsible. If no one is responsible, everyone is innocent and there is no one to sue.

This returns us to our starting place: Is this game worth the candle? An expectation damages regime without the doctrine of excuse locates the risk in exactly one place. This may be an eminently sensible solution, especially among sophisticated parties who are free to transfer the risk if the other is better equipped to bear it. Why not give someone the incentive to look out for risks even if these risks are hard to foresee? It may be much easier for Wolf Trap to obtain insurance than for anyone else in the contractual chain. If it wants to be protected against the unexpected, it can get insurance. It does not have to foresee or specify the events that might force a closing of the theater.

Perhaps for all of these reasons, outside the narrow context of casualty to identified goods, courts are reluctant to find excuse. Wolf Trap will likely fail in its effort to claim that its performance was excused. Weather provides an excuse usually only when it is so bad that the history of climatic variation and other conditions in the particular locality affords no reasonable warning of them. That a storm could knock out power at Wolf Trap was nothing startling. Indeed, it had happened before, although never at the time of the performance.

There seems to be a common thread where excuse is found: (1) expectation damages are not likely to be high; (2) refusing to allow excuse will do little to make the otherwise breaching party take precautions; and (3) the contracting opposite has a substantial ability to mitigate.[16] We want expectation damages to ensure that I take into account your interests in deciding whether to perform. But if my inability to perform is something largely beyond my control, then expectation damages would not have changed my behavior much anyway. In the case of truly extraordinary events, the ordinary damages remedy would give little added incentive to take precautions. We always worry that the duty to mitigate will not do enough to make sure that the innocent party invests the right amount of energy in finding alternatives. The ability to get expectation damages from me may take away from the innocent party the incentive to minimize the costs from the unexpected event. This is always a downside to expectation damages, and it looms large in the classic excuse case.

Return to my Porsche that was struck by lightning after I promised to sell it to you. Given the absence of damages and that there is little likelihood that any legal rule will give me an incentive to take more care than I already have, what matters most is that you have the right set of incentives when you go out looking for the new Porsche. These dynamics are typically at work in those cases in which excuse is found.

7

Duress and the Availability of the Legal Remedy

In any legal system that is imperfect, which is to say in every legal system, we have to worry about advantage taking during the course of the contractual relationship.[1] You are not indifferent between whether I keep my promise to repay your loan or whether I default and you must sue me to recover what you are owed. I can take advantage of these frictions by offering you less than what I owe and make it plain that a long and unpleasant lawsuit awaits if you insist on being paid in full. I extract a modification of our original bargain. I owe you $1,000, but you agree to take the $900 to save yourself the cost and aggravation of suing me. It would seem we should try to prevent such behavior if we could.

But not all demands for contract modification constitute advantage taking. Some renegotiations leave both parties better off. The Great Depression brought with it deflation. It was impossible for some tenants to pay the promised rent, yet no business could enter the same premises and pay more. The old tenant remained the highest valued user, but neither the old tenant nor anyone else could survive at this location with the current rent. It was in the tenant's interest and the landlord's interest to renegotiate the lease and to lower the rent. If the tenant closes the business, the landlord will lose much more than if the lease is renegotiated.

Richard Posner, like Holmes, has made many important contributions to our understanding of the law, both as a judge and as a scholar. Chapter 4 centered around his elucidation of the expectation damages principle. In Chapter 5, we looked at his conception of "good faith" between parties to a contract in his opinion in *Market Street*. In this chapter, we see how his work on the bench illuminates the issue of economic duress. The challenge is one of getting out of the box in which a rigid conception of the doctrine of consideration places us.

Nineteenth-century formalists conflated the question of what was necessary to make a contract enforceable in the first instance with the question of what was needed to modify an existing contract. They assumed that if consideration was required for the former, it was required for the latter as well.[2] This was a mistake. The doctrine of consideration does nothing to help us with the problem we are confronting, which is distinguishing between the problem of my taking advantage of your inability to get true expectation damages if I break my promises and the problem of renegotiating when conditions change.

The risk seems especially large when one manufacturer relies on another for a crucial component.[3] At the last minute, the supplier demands a higher price knowing that no one else can deliver the needed parts on time. It extracts a better deal even though nothing justifies this. Enforcing new terms under such circumstances ultimately makes both parties worse off. When I cannot prevent you from holding me up, I cannot rely on your promise as much in the first instance, and it is therefore less valuable. Equipment makers will pay less, use less efficient means of production (such as vertical integration), and make fewer supplier-specific investments:

> It undermines the institution of contract to allow a contract party to use the threat of breach to get the contract modified in his favor not because anything has happened to require modification in the mutual interest of the parties but simply because the other party, unless he knuckles under to the threat, will incur costs for which he will have no adequate legal remedy.[4]

Because renegotiation is in the mutual self-interest of both parties, the law of contracts faces the challenge of distinguishing between opportunistic holdups on the one hand and mutually beneficial renegotiations on the other.

Posner offers his most interesting exploration of the doctrine in *Oxxford Clothes XX v. Expeditors International of Washington, Inc.*[5] Oxxford Clothes made expensive suits for men out of imported cloth. It defaulted to its largest creditor, one that had a lien on all of its assets. The managers and this creditor reached a deal with one another. The creditor foreclosed on the assets and transferred them to a newly formed corporation ("Oxxford Clothes XX, Inc."). The new corporation carried on exactly the same business as the old one. It looked the same. The new entity, however, was not liable for the debts of the old.

The old creditors of Oxxford Clothes, Inc., were left out in the cold. One of these was Expeditors, a firm that specialized in clearing goods through customs. The new entity—one that appeared to the outside world the same as the old—asked Expeditors to clear new cloth through customs. Expeditors did as it was asked but then refused to turn the cloth over until it was paid everything that the old entity (Oxxford Clothes, Inc.) owed it.

Oxxford XX sued Expeditors in federal court. Oxxford sought a preliminary injunction, but the district judge refused to issue it. At this point, because it could not meet its obligations to major retailers without the cloth, Oxxford XX gave in to Expeditors' demands and paid what the old corporation owed. After it got possession of the cloth, Oxxford XX went back to court demanding that Expeditors return the money on the ground that the payment had been extracted from it under duress. The case finally made its way to the Seventh Circuit and Richard Posner.

Posner begins with *Alaska Packers' Association v. Domenico*,[6] an admiralty case decided by the Ninth Circuit at the start of the last century. The case is rarely cited.[7] The young associate or law clerk trolling through Westlaw looks for recently decided cases with similar facts. For them, *Alaska Packers'* is ancient and irrelevant. But for Posner the case is the archetype that allows him to identify the crucial features of the case before him.

In *Alaska Packers'*, the appellate court recounts how a group of fishermen recruited to work for a season in Alaska refused to fish without a pay increase. Their employer gave in to their demands but then refused to pay once the season was over. The fishermen sued, and the court held the renegotiated deal unenforceable. In return for the promise to increase wages, the fishermen gave nothing. They agreed to do only what they were already legally obliged to do. Hence, the employer's promise was not given in exchange for anything. It was without consideration and therefore unenforceable.

It takes little reflection to see that resolving the case using the doctrine of consideration is of little use in separating those situations in which the renegotiation is value enhancing from those in which it is not. The tenant hit by the Great Depression and the supplier who sees an opportunity to jack up his price are both under a preexisting duty to perform. The change in contract terms is not in exchange for any new consideration in either case, even though the modification is mutually beneficial in the first case and the result of advantage taking in the second.

Moreover, even if an absence of consideration somehow distinguished the two cases, it will do little to curb misbehavior. It is trivially easy to circumvent. If the principle embedded in *Alaska Packers'* were merely about consideration, the fishermen could make the same demand the next time but offer some small change in their promise (such as working one day or one hour or one minute longer) in exchange for the promise of higher wages. Any increased burden would provide sufficient consideration under classical doctrine.

But for Posner as both judge and scholar, one must go beyond the language of the opinion. The true ground of the decision is duress:

> Although the technical ground of decision was the absence of fresh consideration for the modified agreement, it seems apparent . . . that the court's underlying concern was that the modified agreement had been procured by duress in the form of the threat to break the original contract.[8]

To gain some traction on this question, Posner makes his reliance on economic principles explicit: "Duress, understood most concretely, is the situation in which one person obtains a temporary monopoly that it tries to use to obtain a benefit to which it is not entitled."[9] It might seem this observation does not take us that much further. How does one show how the other was trying to capture "a benefit to which it was not entitled"? Why is the tenant during the Great Depression "entitled" to ask for a break from an otherwise binding contact, but the supplier of a crucial part is not?

Economics provides some help here, of course. Some renegotiated deals are value enhancing and others are not. In our Depression hypothetical, the tenant could not stay in business under the terms of the original lease. The renegotiation did not merely redistribute wealth between the parties but also ensured that assets were put to their highest valued use. Even the landlord was better off with the new contract, as no one could operate under the terms of the existing lease. Nevertheless, distinguishing value-enhancing renegotiations from others is hard, at least if the party engaged in opportunism exercises some modest imagination. Even outright extortion is usually done with a certain amount of indirection. The gangster does not say he will break your shop window unless he is paid off. Instead, he offers you "protection" from such mishaps in return for a fee. Hypocrisy is the deference vice pays to virtue.

Focusing on duress does not make even a case such as *Alaska Packers'* easy, as even a cursory examination of the record in that case makes plain.[10] The fishermen in *Alaska Packers'* may not have engaged in extortion at all. They asserted that the nets they were given were defective.

Because their pay was geared to the number of fish they caught, they might well have had legitimate grounds for complaint if the equipment they were given was not what they expected. Indeed, if the packers had promised serviceable nets and these nets were not serviceable, it would be the packers who were in breach. The fishermen would have been entitled to cease performance. A new contract in which the fishermen agreed to work with defective nets in return for higher wages would be entirely enforceable.

In rejecting the fishermen's account of conditions in Alaska, the Ninth Circuit relied in part on the intuition that the packer had every incentive to provide good nets. But the judge who wrote *Economic Analysis of Law* cannot accept such intuitions uncritically, and like many untutored intuitions, this one is flawed. A trade-off must be made between the costs of buying new nets and the costs of fishing with older, less efficient ones. The packer bore all the costs associated with acquiring new nets but did not enjoy all of the benefits of using them, given that the fishermen were paid on the basis of the number of fish they caught.

Moreover, although the fishermen had an incentive to catch as many fish as possible, the packer had an upper limit on the number of fish it could use. It had the supplies necessary to can only a given number of salmon and had no use for the excess. The packer needed a certain number of the fishermen to man the ships back and forth to San Francisco. This task may itself have required so many men that, even with substandard nets, they would have caught enough to meet the capacity of the plant. The packer might have had no need to provide them with decent equipment.

There is an additional wrinkle. This fishery departed from customary practice. It used old nets in combination with new nets, and other fisheries in Alaska did not. The packer claimed that unique conditions at this fishery justified this departure from convention. Even assuming that this was true, however, the packer may have had a duty to disclose. When the packer promised to provide nets, it might have been obliged, unless it said otherwise, to provide nets of the type ordinarily used.

Even if it had no such obligation, this case might be one of mistake. Instead of one party thinking it had a contract for February cotton and the other for April cotton, here one side of the transaction thought they were supposed to fish with new nets and the other thought they would use old nets in combination with new ones. Each side reasonably thought that the bargain was for a different type of net. If each was entitled to use "net" as it was understood in their community, the mistake may have prevented an objective meeting of the minds and kept an enforceable contract from coming into being. If there were no enforceable contract in the first place, any deal struck in Alaska would stand on its own. It would constitute a bargained-for exchange in its own right. The promises made there would represent new obligations each undertook in exchange for the promise of the other.

The Ninth Circuit also likely misunderstood the bargaining dynamic. The amount of bargaining power that the fishermen enjoyed was modest. The court assumed that a strike would expose the packer to heavy losses. This was not true.

The packer relied on native fishermen in addition to those who manned the ship. Even if the men under contract did no fishing at all, the season's catch would not be entirely lost. Moreover, the Alaska Packers' Association was a cartel and, as such, artificially limited the supply of salmon. It was in the process of shutting down its least efficient canneries and would soon close the one involved in this case. Even if no salmon were caught from this cannery, the packer could make up the deficit either by increasing output or releasing more of the surplus catch from previous years to the market.

By contrast, the fishermen found themselves thousands of miles from home and counted on the packer to provide food and housing. Their dependence on the packer further constrained them from acting opportunistically. The packer may also have had the ability to control naked opportunism on the part of the fishermen by its ability to blackball them in subsequent seasons. To be sure, the packer cannot make threats idly. The packer needed to recruit additional fishermen in subsequent years. Nevertheless, these efforts would not be compromised as long as others could distinguish situations in which the packer was retaliating against the fishermen for their own opportunistic behavior from those in which it was behaving opportunistically itself.

Such messy factual inquiries, however, are unnecessary to resolve a case such as *Oxxford*. For Posner, the essential lesson of *Alaska Packers'* is that the packer's claim was plausible only because it had no access to a court at the time the fishermen demanded higher pay. Regardless of the ultimate merits, the case stands for the proposition that every duress case must contain an essential ingredient—a situational monopoly. When it is missing, the claim of duress can be rejected. Whether it actually existed under the facts of *Alaska Packers'* is independent of the principle itself. With respect to any claim of duress, there must be a situational monopoly.

A situational monopoly can exist only if the party claiming duress now in court once did not have access to the court: "The hallmark of duress or extortion is that the victim has no feasible legal remedy."[11] This distinguishes *Alaska Packers'* from many other cases—including *Oxxford*—in which duress is alleged.

> The promise had been made under duress because the defendant had had no feasible remedy against the seamen's demand. It could not have "covered" by hiring substitute seamen on the spot, given the brevity of the Alaska salmon season and the limited supply of seamen in Alaska. And it would not have been feasible for it to sue them, as the filing of many suits would have been necessary and the chances of collecting a significant judgment from each seaman at reasonable cost would have been remote.[12]

Oxxford's action for duress fails because, unlike the packer, the doors of the courthouse were always open to it. Even if one accepts the allegations of the complaint—that Expeditors had utterly no leg to stand on and was acting entirely improperly in holding on to the cloth—Oxxford should lose. Oxxford could invoke (and indeed had invoked) an entirely feasible legal remedy, the preliminary injunction. Its failure to appeal once it lost in the district court was inexplicable.[13]

By zeroing in on the question of whether the aggrieved party had access to the legal system, Posner provides a rule that resolves most cases. Only in hard cases, such as *Alaska Packers'*, where going to court is not an option, does one have to engage in the hard inquiry of whether what is happening is genuine duress or whether it is a reasonable effort to renegotiate in light of changed circumstances.

Under Posner's approach, it is unnecessary to ask whether advantage taking is going on in the vast majority of cases. As long as the aggrieved parties had a courthouse available to them at the time of the threat, we never reach the issue. Among the various economic principles at work in cases of alleged economic duress, Posner focuses on the one that is both easy to decide and that disposes of most of the cases.

Beyond the inaccessibility of the court, the facts of *Alaska Packers'* are not that important. Indeed, over time, Posner's recounting of the facts of *Alaska Packers'* has become increasingly distant from those in the case. The fishermen become sailors on a boat trying to coerce the captain, as opposed to fishermen encamped in a barracks trying to deal with an in-experienced agent.[14]

Posner's approach—as powerful and useful as it is—may partially obscure a problem that is deeply embedded in any system of civil justice.[15] What does it mean to say that a judicial remedy is not available? *Alaska Packers'* is a case that arose in a world in which the courts were weeks or months away. When is this ever going to happen today? Technological innovation has reduced the distance to the courthouse for everyone. A legal right exists only to the extent that the law protects it with an effective remedy. If someone succumbs to a demand today because there is no remedy that protects her rights, in what sense can one say that the individual possesses those rights in the first instance? For a judge such as Posner, the answer is simple: not very often.

To recognize duress in a case such as *Oxxford,* one needs to explain why preliminary relief was not available. If we accept (as Posner does for purposes of analyzing the duress question) that Expeditors had no right to keep the cloth at all, Oxxford should have been able to obtain preliminary relief. Expeditors asserted it had only a lien in the cloth. Hence, by its own account, its only right in the cloth was the right to be paid a fixed sum. The judge need require Oxxford only to post a bond as a condition of granting preliminary relief to protect Expeditors fully from the risk that Oxxford would ultimately lose. There were few costs to granting a preliminary injunction. There was no harm to Expeditors from granting the preliminary injunction even if it turned out later to be issued erroneously, and there was a substantial benefit to Oxxford if it ended up winning. Under these circumstances, the district court's refusal to grant the preliminary injunction seems wrong.[16]

For Posner, however, an error on the part of the district judge makes no difference. Posner appears quite inclined to accept the idea that the district court should have issued the injunction. Without quite saying so, he leaves the impression that the district court blundered: Expeditors made silly noises about having a lien on the cloth, and the judge thought such an argument both meritorious and sufficient when it was likely neither. But error on the part of the district court is irrelevant.

Oxxford could have appealed to the Seventh Circuit. Some appellate courts would not be able to respond within the few days that Oxxford needed relief, but the Seventh Circuit under Posner was an exception.[17] Moreover, the ability to appeal should not matter. Duress is not a doctrine designed to protect litigants from judicial error. The right to bring a duress action in the face of a stupid judicial decision is little more than the right to bring the same civil action again if the first judge decides incorrectly. Finality is an essential feature of all civil justice systems, all of which are imperfect to some degree.

If the district court was correct in denying the preliminary injunction, the case of duress is weaker still. Duress should not be available merely because of the inadequacy of the relief the court is otherwise empowered to provide. The standard remedy for breach of contract—expectation damages—is systematically undercompensatory, at least in practice. But a shortfall in the protection contract law provides for victims of breach of promise is not a reason to apply the doctrine of duress. The deficiency is a feature of the law that must be assessed on its own terms. If it is inadequate, it should be changed directly, not through the backdoor.

When preliminary relief is not available, the legal system has made the judgment, right or wrong, that suing for damages after the fact is sufficient. The mechanism the law puts in place to vindicate a given right cannot be separated from the right itself. Introducing duress in such situations merely second-guesses a decision already embedded in the law about the protection that should be afforded someone who calls on the power of the state to enforce a promise.

Posner has never written an opinion in which he found duress available to a litigant. But for the Young Astronomer—whether Holmes or Posner—what matters are the judgments he issues, whether he writes the opinion or joins one written by another judge. The job of the legal pragmatist is one of mapping the judgments that emerge from litigated disputes. Hence, to provide an assessment of Posner's approach to duress, we need to cast the net more broadly and look at all the economic duress cases in which he was on the panel. When we do this, we can find one case in which he joined an opinion in which a renegotiated agreement was held not to be enforceable.

In *Contempo Design, Inc. v. Council of Carpenters*,[18] the employer and the union agreed to abide by the terms of an industry-wide collective bargaining agreement unless either chose to opt out and give the other three months' notice. The agreement included a no-strike clause. Without giving the proper notice, the workers demanded new terms and went on strike to secure them. The strike caught Contempo at a time when it was courting a large new customer and facing financial pressure from its banks. It succumbed to the workers' demands and then sought to have the new contract rescinded.

The court found in favor of Contempo. It adopted the same rationale as *Alaska Packers'*. The new contract was not supported by any additional consideration. The workers were already bound to perform under the collective bargaining agreement. Promising to do what one is already legally obliged to do is not sufficient consideration to support a promise.

This opinion, in which Posner joined, merely rehearses blackletter law and focuses narrowly on the unenforceability of a contract in which there is no modification of the original duties, however trivial. Posner, as a judge bound by state court interpretations of the common law, may have felt bound to follow cases that were tied narrowly to the doctrine of consideration. This seems unlikely, however. When writing his own opinions, looking at the same precedent, Posner never found that absence of consideration key. All his opinions, even when based on state law, emphasize the situational monopoly.

There may be an explanation for why Posner finds duress in *Contempo Design* but not *Oxxford*. The difficulty the employer faced in *Contempo* was different from the one in *Oxxford*. Under the Norris-LaGuardia Act, federal courts lack the power to issue an injunction against a strike. It might seem that this should make no difference. Contempo's inability to obtain a preliminary injunction reflects a judgment that the ordinary damage remedy was adequate.

But there may be a difference between *Contempo* and the typical case. The inability of a court to enforce the employer's rights stems from a congressional policy unrelated to the substantive rights of the parties. Congress put a limit on judicial power in order to bring about labor peace. It is not a judgment about the merits of the employer's legal rights or the adequacy of its legal remedy. The inability to stop the strike derives from a legislative decision unconnected with the relief to which an employer is later entitled after the fact. It is not like a decision that expectation damages is the appropriate remedy for the injury suffered.

The postmodern doctrine of duress, as shaped by Posner, ultimately turns on the availability of the judicial remedy and more specifically on the nature of what is constraining its availability. Distance from the courthouse or an inability to appear before the court once might have created the situational monopoly that the doctrine requires, but few parties will ever find themselves out of touch with a court today. Little else remains. Duress should not be available merely because the legislature protects a substantive right with a modest remedy. Duress is not an avenue to expand legal rights. Someone claiming duress must show that the court's inability to grant preliminary relief arises from a circumstance or policy unconnected with the legal right itself. These do not exist very often, as the limits on the power to enjoin are rarely subject to special constraints analogous to those in the Norris-LaGuardia Act.

Under this view, a case such as *Austin Instrument, Inc. v. Loral Corp.* may not be rightly decided.[19] The supplier threatened to hold up the shipment of parts the buyer needed to meet its own contractual obligations. But the holdup power arose only because the buyer's damage remedy was undercompensatory. This is not a problem that duress is designed to fix. If specific relief (and a preliminary injunction) were not available, it would seem the buyer's problem was with the modest remedy the law chooses to give, not with its inability to go to court.

A claim of duress should not be available to compensate someone for the benefit she would have received if a preliminary injunction had been available. If one were entitled to a preliminary injunction, one should have asked for it. If one asked for it and relief was denied in error, it should still make no difference. Such errors are part of any legal system. And if one were not entitled to a preliminary injunction in the first place, granting a claim of duress makes even less sense. The lack of a preliminary remedy reflects a decision that the subsequent damage action is sufficient. Unless the court is denied the power to act for reasons unconnected with the legal right, recognizing a claim of duress merely becomes a backdoor way of obtaining more relief than the legal system has deemed appropriate. Such is the way Posner has made sense of the doctrine of economic duress.

Oxxford Fabrics illustrates the way in which Richard Posner has harnessed the tools of economics to make him a common law judge of great distinction. By focusing attention first on such questions as whether the purported victim of duress had access to the court, he ensures that lower-court judges can resolve disputes in ways that both make sense and are consistent with decided precedent. Ironically, he is not using the tools of the Young Astronomer, or at least not in the same way. Instead of being the objective observer trying to understand the deep structure of the legal cosmos, he is immersed in the quotidian task of supervising dozens of lower-court judges of sometimes-limited competence. Posner as a judge is a pragmatist in an altogether different sense.

Posner captures the narrowest view of duress in its modern guise. Your ability to make a claim for duress turns crucially on your ability to explain why you were unable to vindicate your rights by going to court and obtaining relief at the time you were threatened. If you claim duress, you cannot win by talking about consideration or abstract notions of fairness. The burden is on you to explain why, given the availability of the courthouse, you caved in. If you are in Alaska in 1900 and the nearest judge is hundreds of miles away, that is one thing. But if you are in Chicago and the federal courts are open for business and able to grant exactly the type of relief you seek, do not expect to be able to come and complain about it later if you did not obtain such relief—or if you tried and failed.

Legal systems are necessarily resource constrained. The party who claims "duress" must do more than claim that, in the absence of such relief, it will not be made entirely whole. If the problem is that an award of expectation damages in practice fails to force the person who breaks her promise to internalize the costs of my breach, we either have to change the way we measure damages, offer a different remedy, or content ourselves with a remedy that falls somewhat short. But this is where the focus should be. It has nothing to do with "duress," let alone consideration.

A more expansive view of duress than Posner's still places a heavy burden on the person claiming duress after the fact to show why she did not go to court in the first place. There has to be something more than a generic complaint about the speed of the process or the effectiveness of the legal remedy.

8

Fine Print: Contracts in Mass Markets

For many decades, contracts scholars have worried about enforcing form contracts from standardized transactions in the marketplace.[1] Many consumers enter into contracts that run for many pages or screens, and few bother to read them. Holding people to these terms seems wholly foreign to the idea of contracts being the domain of a voluntary exchange of promises. It is hard to say someone has made a promise when it is embedded in fine print that the person has never read and that no one seriously expects her to read. It would seem there is a potential for advantage taking, and a sensible law of contracts must concern itself with this.

Before we even reach the question of contract law, however, we have to recognize that contract law itself is only a small part of the legal system. Legal rules outside of contract constrain those who are tempted to play games with fine print. A seller cannot promise the moon during the course of selling a product and then seek to escape legal liability by adding terms in forms. We do not need to resolve any questions about the effectiveness of disclaimers or the parol evidence rule. Rules governing false advertising and fraud prevent such deliberate misconduct.[2] The buyer can prevail without having to assert any rights under the contract. Even if the consumer would not have any cause of action based on breach of contract, sellers are still held in check.

The most outrageous forms of abuse are subject to criminal sanctions. But quite apart from the criminal law, merchants have always operated in heavily regulated environments. At medieval fairs, there were many rules ensuring that goods were publicly displayed and weights and measures were subject to inspection. In our own time, elaborate regulations protect buyers of everything from commercial jets to candy bars. These regulations focus on particular products and particular types of transactions.

Regulation targeted at payday lending[3] or door-to-door sales[4] focus on discrete transactions involving particularly vulnerable buyers. We should expect these to do more heavy lifting than contract doctrines that apply uniformly to every sort of transaction.

Of course, we should not dismiss the role that contract law can play merely because other laws are at work. But we do need to worry that by focusing our attention on a particular issue—in this case the potential abuse by the use of standardized terms in fine print—we may lose the ability to vindicate other goals. The first order of business is to understand the stakes. The problem likely exists in some measure, and ensuring against the worst abuses is prudent, but we need to keep the problem in perspective. Fighting against every form of abuse, real and imagined, may compromise our ability to reach other goals.

Playing games with fine print may not be the source of mischief law professors are sometimes inclined to believe. You make more money by selling people things they do not need than you do by pretending to give them what they want and then taking it away in fine print. Harold Hill in *The Music Man* made his money by persuading towns that they needed a boys' band. He did not seek out places where people already wanted to buy seventy-six trombones and then sell them defective ones. Richard Sears of Sears-Roebuck fame grew rich by selling catalogue goods with money-back guarantees. One of his popular products was the Heidelberg Belt, an electrical device that was buckled around the waist. If the belts did not cure their impotency, buyers were free to return them. Only three ever did. As Sears observed toward the end of his life, "Honesty is the best policy. I know. I've tried it both ways."[5] A vision of commercial law that worries excessively about the ability of parties to sneak terms past each other distracts us from the things that matter.

In particular, we need to be attuned to the possibility that what seems to be troublesome fine print may be a symptom of an altogether different problem. Later in this chapter, I suggest that two of the most important cases involving fine print from the middle of the last century, *Henningsen v. Bloomfield Motors, Inc.*[6] and *Williams v. Walker-Thomas Furniture Co.*,[7] are examples of exactly this. First, I attempt to identify the scope of the problem we face.

Fine Print as a Product Attribute

As lawyers, we must resist the temptation to think that contract law presents a unique set of problems. The advantage an unscrupulous seller might take with respect to contract terms may be no different than many other things. The warranty that comes with your laptop computer is one of its many product attributes. The laptop has a screen of a particular size. Its microprocessors work at a particular speed, and the battery lasts a given amount of time between recharging. The hard drive has a certain capacity and mean time to failure. There is an instruction manual, online technical support (or lack thereof), and software. Then there are the warranties that the seller makes (or does not make) that are also part of the bundle. Just as I know the size of the screen but nothing about the speed of the microprocessor, I know about some of the warranty terms that come with the computer and remain wholly ignorant of others.

With respect to some product attributes, buyers have options. For a higher price, I can buy a computer with a bigger screen. But with respect to others, there is no choice. A seller may offer laptop computers with only one type of battery. Such is also the case with the attributes that are legal terms. A seller may give me a choice: I can buy a service contract that extends the warranty. Other times, there will be no choice, as when the seller specifies that Delaware law governs any contract dispute between us. Similarly, some product attributes are readily apparent to everyone, such as the size of the screen and the availability of an expensive service contract. Other product attributes, like the speed of the microprocessor and the forum selection clause, are apparent only to those who spend time and energy looking for them.

Buyers in mass markets have little choice over the way that a particular seller bundles her product. You could buy Henry Ford's Model T in any color you wanted as long as it was black.[8] The warranty that came with the Model T was the same. You could have any warranty you wanted as long as it was Ford's. The inability to choose is a by-product of mass production. There is more uniformity, but the goods are cheaper. Those who care about color are worse off; the price-conscious are better off. Hidden product attributes over which sellers give potential buyers no choice are commonplace and necessary features of mass markets.

The typical buyer cannot easily rely on her own expertise or her ability to assess products from different sellers. Search costs are high. These costs include not only finding someone who works for the seller who possesses the relevant information but also gaining enough expertise to make sensible judgments about what is revealed. After a buyer discovered that the Model T had a magneto radically different from that in any other car, she still needed to figure out whether it was better or worse than a more conventional design.

When the market works effectively, however, the typical buyer benefits from the presence of other, more sophisticated buyers.[9] A seller in a mass market often cannot distinguish among her buyers. To make a profit, she cannot focus exclusively on the unsophisticated. I am ignorant about computers, but I can see whether the more knowledgeable are buying a particular model. When the seller decides on the microprocessor to use in her new computer, she has to worry about making a choice that suits not only the buyers like me who do not know about microprocessors but also those who do. As long as there are enough sophisticated buyers aware of the importance of having the right microprocessor, the seller must choose well. The sophisticated buyer provides protection for those who are entirely ignorant.

Payday lending is a potential place for useful regulation precisely because of the danger that the borrowers in such a market (those who live from one paycheck to the next) are not likely to include sophisticated parties. One cannot justify regulation on this account alone, but it becomes a factor to consider once one pays attention to the market as a whole.

The law works identically with respect to contract terms and other hidden product attributes. The challenge we face has little to do with how well the typical buyer understands fine print. Instead, the focus should be on what channels are available for buyers with the skill and the inclination to become informed about the product and whether the law makes this process easier or harder. Instead of reading the fine print or disassembling the product herself, the sophisticated buyer might prefer to rely on the seller's representations. The representation about the warranty or microprocessor is credible because the law imposes penalties on sellers that induce truth telling. A law that puts a seller in jail for telling an outright lie makes searching easier. Instead of running her own test on the microprocessor, a sophisticated buyer can ask the seller for technical specifications and tests that the seller has run.

When the law enables the sophisticated buyer to learn about product attributes easily, sellers will be under greater pressure to build computers that meet such a buyer's expectations. There is nothing particularly special about what the law is doing with respect to fine print as opposed to other hidden product attributes, but the law brings benefits to everyone to the extent that it makes it easier for sophisticated buyers to become informed. Promoting this flow of information, however, is not the same as making sure that every buyer is aware of what is buried in fine print.

Of course, there may not be enough sophisticated buyers to give a seller the right incentives. There are computers with microprocessors that are too slow and warranties that are too stingy that are sold to people like me every day. But the question is not whether the market is perfect but how we should shape legal rules to make markets work more effectively.

Some kinds of protection for unsophisticated buyers are worth having because they come at little cost. For example, there are few downsides to making an implied warranty of merchantability hard to waive as long as the warranty provides a baseline that everyone with any knowledge or sophistication would demand. Assuming courts were able to ascertain such things, knowledgeable buyers would insist on a warranty that ensures that the computer passes without objection in the trade and is suitable for the purposes for which such a computer is typically used. Mandatory warranties become problematic only when they include provisions that do not sensibly allocate responsibilities between buyer and seller.

The other steps that should be taken to curtail abuse and otherwise make the market work more effectively are not obvious. Our legal system embodies a general reluctance to review a transaction to assess the fairness of the price at which goods are sold. I can sell a necklace for $15,000, even if others sell virtually the same piece for $10,000. I can sell a laptop computer for the same price as my competitors and not disclose that my disk drive is cheaper, my chips are slower, and my housing is less sturdy. I can charge $5 a fifth for my standard brand of vodka and $10 for the premium brand, even if they come from the same tap.

The law does nothing to prevent someone from taking a product that is not well made (even though it is not so bad as to violate implied warranties or give rise to any other contract remedy) and charge as much as the market will bear. It is in this environment that we must assess how much of a difference contract law can make when it comes to regulating fine print.

Contract Law in a Supporting Role

Contract law affects only those who are around for the long term. Those interested in making a quick killing are likely to be out of the jurisdiction or judgment-proof by the time the law catches up with them. In these cases, causes of action do not matter. Rules governing the fine print matter only when there is enough time for a court to act and grant meaningful relief. Those who are in business for any length of time, however, must worry about their reputations. Hence, the cases in which legal sanctions matter are those in which reputational forces are necessarily also at work. Moreover, parties are most likely to invest in their reputations in environments where the other party fears advantage taking. In the arena in which it operates, contract law governing fine print may be doing little of the heavy lifting. An experience in my own life brought this lesson home to me.

Many years ago, toward the end of his life, my father wanted to give my mother a piece of jewelry on her birthday. An emerald and diamond pin he saw in a Tiffany's catalogue caught his eye, and he clipped out the picture and sent it to Norm, a jeweler with whom he previously had done business. Norm agreed to make a similar pin for a price that, although much less than Tiffany's, was hardly insubstantial. He gave it to my father, who in turn gave it to me to look after until my mother's birthday.

I had never been much impressed with Norm. Norm had a small and somewhat seedy shop, and most of his business was in wholesaling items such as tasteless pins in the shape of an American flag with semiprecious red, white, and blue stones. Moreover, the opportunity for advantage taking was nontrivial. My father was in search of a deal. He wanted a pin like the one from Tiffany's but for less. Additionally, he was quite ill and did not know much about jewelry. He was not in a position to cast a sharp eye on the transaction.

Because of my doubts (and because I interpreted my father's charge to look after the pin broadly), I took it to a well-known jeweler on North Michigan Avenue in Chicago. This jeweler examined the pin closely and, after some study, shook his head and told me he had bad news. Emeralds were a very soft stone and mounting them this way was extremely tricky. Unfortunately (but not surprisingly), two of the emeralds had fractured while being mounted. He handed me a magnifying glass and invited me to see for myself. I thought I saw what he was talking about but was not sure. The jeweler suggested that I return the pin and ask to have the emeralds replaced.

At that moment, I had little hope that Norm would replace the stones. The flaws were invisible or nearly so. I was not sure I could persuade Norm that the fractures were there. Moreover, the price my father paid and the problems with the mount might be connected with each other. We acquired the pin at a favorable price, because the quality was not first-rate. We should not have thought that the pin from Norm would be comparable to one from Tiffany's.

I said as much to the Michigan Avenue jeweler, more or less expecting him to agree and suggest, with some condescension, that, in the future, we should rely on upscale jewelers like him. His response, however, was nothing of the sort. A dark look came over him, as if I had impugned his entire profession. "Your jeweler *will* replace the stones. I am not talking about the design or the quality of the stones. The emeralds have fractures in them. It doesn't matter what you paid. A jeweler would never knowingly let such a pin leave his store. *Never.*"

I did not have to explain to Norm why I was returning the pin. He took some time to collect his thoughts, and then he talked to me. He needed to apologize. He had let my father down. The emeralds had fractures in them, and the pin should never have left the shop. The fault, he told me, was entirely his. He had not personally inspected the pin. This had been his practice for decades, but of late he had started to delegate too much business to his sons. They were not ready. Then he asked for the date of my mother's birthday. He needed to find new stones and wanted to be sure the pin was ready in time.

Like other merchants, jewelers are constrained by powerful customs of the trade. Norm's shop was seedy because he was largely in the wholesale business. The jeweler on North Michigan Avenue had a fancy shop and a reputation. All Norm had was his reputation. Jewelers have to care intensely about their reputations precisely because their goods are hard to assess. The same force that made us vulnerable (our inability to judge the pin on our own) also made it much more important for Norm to build a reputation that is put at risk if commercial customs are broken.

We need to assess default rules such as the implied warranty of merchantability against this backdrop. It might have been possible to bring an action against Norm if he refused to replace the emeralds. The pin, after all, did not pass without objection in the trade. But the same custom that gave rise to the legal right made it unnecessary. For all I knew, Norm had a form that disclaimed the implied warranty of merchantability, but such a disclaimer was irrelevant as long as reputational forces ensured that he would make amends if his goods did not pass in his trade.

In addition to the need to preserve a reputation for fair dealing, other forces are at work. Among the most important are criminal sanctions. A jeweler in Norm's position could, in theory, have provided us with fake stones and escaped detection most of the time. Similarly, he could have provided stones that weighed less or were of a different grade than he represented. These forms of advantage taking, however, rely on affirmative misrepresentations that give someone in Norm's position legal problems quite independent of contract law. It takes only one customer to get a second opinion for the entire business to unravel. Rules governing forms matter only if the contracting party is around long enough to be subject to the legal process but not constrained by commercial custom.

The Fine Art of the Short Con

One way to assess the potential for advantage taking through the use of fine print is to look at the motivations of those inclined to mischief. The advantage taking of concern to us is analogous to an unscrupulous seller offering insurance to the unsophisticated. The limitations on coverage in the fine print are not contrary to what the seller represented, but in the aggregate they insulate the insurer from liability in the cases that matter. Most people who buy the lousy insurance never file any claims. They are none the wiser. The few that make claims discover that they are not covered, but they think it their bad luck to have suffered a misfortune that was beyond the coverage of the policy. They usually go away quietly as well.

"Big cons" are confidence games in which a single individual is separated from a lot of money. They depend crucially on finding rich people willing to enter schemes that are illicit in one way or another. By contrast, playing games with fine print is a "short con."[10] One gets rich by cheating many people a little bit at a time. We want to ask whether a master of the short con naturally gravitates toward playing games with fine print, a space in which a seller offers substandard products or services and tries to escape responsibility when things go badly. The idea is to make money, not by making a big lie, but by appearing to promise one thing while actually promising far less. The advantage taking is too small to be stopped by reputational forces and too venial to fall within criminal and regulatory sanctions.

Once when veteran bank robber Willie Sutton was arrested, a reporter asked why he robbed banks. Willie told him, "That's where the money is." If one wants to take advantage of people and profit by it, one naturally looks to arenas that promise the most in the way of profits. Fine print may not be such a venue.

We can return to my experience with Norm. If Norm had been inclined toward sharp practices, he had many chances to take advantage of my father without disclaiming legal obligations. The pin was custom-made. My father had no benchmark other than the Tiffany's price to assess whether Norm was charging a fair price. If Norm were inclined to take advantage of my father, he simply could have charged more for it.

Alternatively, he could have used cheaper stones or lower-quality mounts. These avenues would not have put his reputation at risk to nearly the same extent.

The key to playing any con game is ensuring that the deception lasts long enough. A large part of the swindler's craft lies in his ability to do this. It is known as "cooling out the mark": "If the insideman handles the blow-off properly, the mark hardly knows he has been fleeced. No good insideman wants any trouble with a mark. He wants him to lose his money the 'easy way' rather than the 'hard way.' "[11] When one is engaged in a less-than-honorable transaction in the marketplace, keeping marks happy is especially important. The best cons are the ones in which the marks never know that they have been swindled. It is not as hard as it might seem. People want to believe that they have received a good deal. They do not want to think that they have been duped. Even when they know they have been cheated, they do not want others to know and are reluctant to invoke whatever legal rights they have on that account.

To return to the example of the emerald pin, let us assume that we have a jeweler with bad motives. In addition to, or instead of, using inferior stones and other tactics that do not violate any implied terms, this jeweler wants to profit by selling jewels with fractures in them. Such a jeweler can rely in the first place on most buyers never checking the goods out. Among other things, buyers, as a general matter, believe in their own powers of judgment. The spouse that receives the pin as a birthday gift is unlikely to have suspicions either. Even when buyers have suspicions, the unscrupulous often can allay them, especially with respect to details (such as nearly invisible fractures) that require expertise.

The worst-case scenario may be one in which a third party enters the picture unexpectedly, such as an overeager lawyer-academic possessed of a strong sense of filial obligation, a large amount of suspicion, and plenty of free time. Even in this case, however, the unscrupulous need not rely on legal niceties. In such cases, they may be better off fixing (or pretending to fix) the defect, rather than insisting that they do not have to. Fine print is not playing a role in any of this.

A seller profits from using tricky fine print only when buyers use the product and discover that it does not work and would otherwise seek recourse against the seller. If you plan to cheat someone and disappear, you do not need fine print. Fine print is only useful for sellers who are around for the long term, and the buyer would otherwise seek recourse against them. Buyers invoke their rights under implied terms such as the warranty of merchantability only if they know that their goods are defective. If there are express promises, disclaimers of off-the-rack terms are irrelevant. If the buyer never notices the defect, the implied warranty does the buyer no good. Even if the buyer learns about the defect, the warranty again matters only if the seller insists on holding the buyer to the preprinted forms. To win with fine print, the unscrupulous must ultimately be willing to invoke defenses such as disclaimers and remedy limitations in open court. Con men, however, rarely want to do this and in any event cannot count on success, quite apart from the letter of the law.

Sellers inclined to mischief will direct their attention to the places where the potential gains are the largest and the costs smallest. By this standard, fine print is an exceedingly poor candidate for would-be advantage takers. Not only is the ability to exploit fine print smaller than it might first seem, but the stakes may also be quite low. For most goods, the chance of defects that give rise to warranty actions, and the like, is comparatively small. The "insurance" that implied terms provide is only a fraction of the total package. With few goods is it likely to be worth even 10 percent of the price of the goods.

A seller intent on taking advantage of buyers should have many better ways of shortchanging buyers other than playing with fine print. Goods that are fungible are easy to inspect, and hence the implied warranty matters little. For complex goods such as computers, it is easy to use low-quality materials and shave costs in this way, rather than try to use fine print. In some markets, buyers may be sensitive to product attributes, but they are likely to ask about warranties as well, and as we have seen, affirmative misrepresentations about these independently trigger legal liability.

Even when warranties matter, it does not follow that badly motivated sellers seek to avoid them. Quite the contrary. Just as an unscrupulous seller can provide second-rate (but merchantable) goods at a premium price, the same seller can provide a second-rate warranty (often called a "service contract") at a premium price. It is far easier and more profitable to build a reliable computer and convince a naive consumer to buy an overpriced service contract that she will never use than to build an inferior computer and rely on fine print when the buyer comes to complain.

The successful con artist usually identifies a discrete set of people who are vulnerable. Mass marketing goods to the world at large does not allow one to do this. It is sometimes thought that consumers are worse off when they buy in a mass market and are forced to take terms on a take-it-or-leave-it basis. In many cases, exactly the opposite is true. An unscrupulous seller has a hard time taking advantage of the ignorant if they are buying the same goods in the same marketplace as Fortune 500 companies.

Unsophisticated consumers are better off in a market in which no one can bargain for special terms than in a market where everyone can. I am more likely to enjoy terms that are mutually beneficial when I buy a computer with terms that the manufacturer imposes on everyone, including large companies, than when I and every other customer can dicker with the same manufacturer individually.

Regulation of the Marketplace

In *Henningsen v. Bloomfield Motors, Inc.,*[12] the buyers of a car sued a carmaker for the consequential damages from an accident caused by a defective steering mechanism. By their account, the car had been traveling on a smooth, paved highway at twenty miles an hour. Suddenly, there was a loud noise. The steering wheel spun, and the car veered and crashed into a highway sign and a brick wall. The front of the car was so badly damaged that it was impossible to determine whether any of the parts of the steering wheel mechanism or workmanship or assembly were defective before the accident.[13]

The carmaker defended on the ground that the buyers waived any right to sue for consequential damages in fine print.[14] The court ruled in favor of the buyers, holding the waiver ineffective. The court focused on "[t]he gross inequality of bargaining position"[15] and explained:

> The traditional contract is the result of free bargaining of parties who are brought together by the play of the market, and who meet each other on a footing of approximate economic equality. In such a society there is no danger that freedom of contract will be a threat to the social order as a whole. But in present-day commercial life the standardized mass contract has appeared. It is used primarily by enterprises with strong bargaining power and position.[16]

After six decades, this reasoning seems both dated and economically naive. Mass markets produce standardized products with standardized terms. Standardization has nothing to do with bargaining power. All carmakers sell cars with four wheels, rather than three or five. Anyone who wants to buy a car has to buy one with four wheels on a take-it-or-leave-it basis. We could mandate the production of three-wheeled or five-wheeled cars, but we should have a better reason than superior bargaining power or armchair notions of car design. The same is true of a warranty. As noted, a warranty is a product attribute, and the type of warranty suitable for any given product is not self-evident.

Although not the focus of the opinion, the court does observe that the carmaker used a standard warranty issued by the Automobile Manufacturers Association.[17] Standing alone, a standard warranty is not problematic either. There are economies of scale in developing contract terms. A trade association can call on the collective expertise of everyone in the business to develop an efficient set of terms. If it does a good job, everyone will use these terms. If it does a bad job, no one will. Even a monopolist looks for efficient warranty terms. Using inefficient terms compromises the monopolist's ability to extract rents. She is much better off providing quality goods and efficient terms and charging as much as she can from them.

Trade associations, however, create opportunities for anticompetitive behavior.[18] When sellers in an industry enter into a cartel agreement and agree to fix prices, each must monitor the others. Every cartel member has an incentive to cheat by lowering prices and gaining a higher market share for itself.

When goods are as complex as a car, the ability to change the quality of the goods increases the monitoring problem. Raising the quality of the goods has the same effect as lowering the price. It allows one member of the cartel to gain market share at the expense of the others. Hence, members of such a cartel would like to devise mechanisms to minimize cheating over this dimension. A standardized warranty suits this purpose admirably.

When each member of the cartel agrees to use the same warranty and to bind its dealers never to go beyond it, they can no longer use a warranty to signal product quality.[19] With less ability to signal quality, they have less incentive to compete over product quality. To be sure, members of the cartel have no reason to choose a warranty that is suboptimal, but they do want their agreed-upon warranty to be one that can be easily monitored. Uniform and simple warranties might emerge in such environments. These are not necessarily inefficient, but they are not necessarily efficient either.

At the time of *Henningsen,* three manufacturers made substantially all of the cars sold in the United States, and they entered an explicit agreement to provide the same warranty to all their customers and to require their dealers to do the same.[20] The minutes survive from the meeting in which this agreement was discussed and voted on. There does not seem to have been an explicit price-fixing cartel, but tacit collusion can easily arise in such environments. We ought to be on our guard when the members of the industry reach an explicit agreement with each other about anything. Such agreements make tacit collusion easier. Again, the problem here was not that General Motors, Ford, and Chrysler used the same warranty (the vice the court in *Henningsen* focused on) but that they bound themselves to use the same warranty.

One cannot say for certain that this agreement among carmakers in the automobile industry was intended to facilitate a scheme that left the industry less competitive, but it is plausible that it did. In any event, it is hard to see how barring such explicit agreements could leave consumers worse off. In short, the standardized warranty in *Henningsen* is suspect. The problem, however, has nothing to do with lack of sophistication or an inability to bargain. An infinitely sophisticated and savvy car purchaser, completely aware of every term of the warranty, is as subject to cartel behavior as anyone else.

But this does not mean that if carmakers vigorously competed with respect to warranties that the plaintiff in *Henningsen* would have received the promise she sought—liability for consequential damages. It does not seem implausible that a carmaker even in a highly competitive market would disclaim liability for consequential damages. The driver will carry insurance. Although it is possible that the steering mechanism was defective, it is also possible that something else caused the accident. In a world in which juries resolve factual disputes, consumers may be better off accepting a disclaimer rather than paying the higher price that covers the cost of paying for accidents caused by the carelessness of others but for which a jury will hold the carmaker liable.

Carmakers may disclaim liability for consequential damages because it represents a sensible trade-off between the risks that the carmaker is equipped to bear and those the consumer can bear.[21] Liability for consequential damages is regularly and consistently disclaimed, across all products in all markets against all types of buyers of whatever sophistication. Buyers may be better positioned to guard against them than sellers. There is little to suggest that a carmaker would ever make this promise, no matter what the bargaining environment was. A sophisticated buyer with bargaining power does not demand a promise that she values less than it costs the seller.

Fine Print and Paternalism

For centuries, our law has provided that creditors in ordinary run-of-the-mill transactions do not acquire the right to reach wedding rings, family bibles, the clothes on their debtor's backs, or their basic necessities. This is a sensible background rule. Given the high value we place on having such assets, the most deliberate among us would seldom put these assets at risk. We would rather pay higher interest rates at the outset than face these risks after the fact. Those of us who do not act so deliberately might be tempted to put such property at risk, but only because we do not appreciate the potential consequences.

Giving individuals private rights of action is a serious business. We are allowing private individuals to call on the state to use force, if necessary, against another private individual. This is especially true in the context of debtor-creditor relations. There is nothing foreordained about the extent to which creditors should be able to call on the state to collect their debts, and the rights extended here have always been carefully limited.

The law denies creditors the ability to reach some assets when we default in part because we are too inclined to make borrowing decisions without taking full account of the long-term consequences at the time we borrow. We misjudge the likelihood of future hard times. We do not fully realize that, although the chance of any particular reverse of fortune might be small, the chance that at least one such reversal comes to pass is substantial.[22] Moreover, we do not appreciate the value of being able to keep such property in hard times.

The place to draw the line between property that creditors can reach and property they cannot is neither foreordained nor obvious, but there is a difference between a Ferrari, on the one hand, and a wedding ring, on the other. Most individuals can deal with the loss of the former, but they put property of the latter sort at risk in a marketplace transaction only after the most careful consideration and under the most unusual circumstances.

Once property is insulated from creditor levy, we have to decide how to treat security interests in such property. Empowering a debtor to grant a security interest in exempt property has the effect of allowing an individual to waive her right to keep it beyond the reach of creditors. There are reasons to allow such waivers. A wedding ring makes for an excellent hostage.[23] The borrower knows that the creditor has little temptation to abscond with it, while the lender knows that the borrower will go through great lengths to repay the loan and retrieve the ring. By her willingness to put such an asset at risk, an individual debtor can signal her confidence that she can repay her obligations by allowing creditors to reach such assets.

The challenge, however, is allowing individuals to create such security interests without at the same time undercutting one of the rationales that led to exempting the property from creditor levy in the first place. It makes no sense to exempt property from creditor levy to protect debtors from their own inability to assess the chances and consequences of default without worrying at the same time about regulating waivers of the right. If debtors are likely to undervalue the importance of household goods, they will also be too quick to grant a security interest in them.

At the very least, the law needs to ensure that waivers are done with sufficient reflection and deliberation. The law here, in other words, needs to perform what Lon Fuller called a cautionary function.[24] By requiring that a formal ritual accompany the grant of a security interest, we ensure that the debtor reflects on the act and its consequences.

If you want to use your wedding ring as collateral for a loan, it may make sense to insist that you jump through enough hoops so that we can be confident that you have thought carefully about what you are doing. To give a lender a security interest in a wedding ring, you must part with possession of it. An individual can borrow by using her wedding ring as collateral, but she must go to a pawnshop, take the ring off her finger, and hand it over to the pawnbroker.[25]

Such a rule is costly and makes it hard for debtors to create a security interest in their wedding rings, but this is the point. We do not want it to be easy. To ensure that debtors make such decisions deliberately, we need to force them out of their routine. Justifying formal rules in this environment is straightforward once we accept the underlying policy that governs exempt property.

Thinking about exempt property in this fashion allows us to make sense of one of the classic cases involving boilerplate and fine print—*Williams v. Walker-Thomas Furniture*.[26] Williams bought a number of pieces of household furniture from Walker-Thomas for about $1,300.

After having paid all but $164 of this amount, she bought a stereo from Walker-Thomas for $514. The contract she signed included a cross-collateralization clause. This provision gave Walker-Thomas a security interest in both the stereo and all the other furniture she bought from it over the years. The case turned on the question of whether this clause in fine print was enforceable.

To understand the case, one has to understand the work the clause is doing. It is a device that gives Walker-Thomas access to assets that are otherwise out of bounds. Walker-Thomas took the security interest in Williams's other household goods because these assets were exempt. It had to take a security interest in them in order to be able to reach them in the event of default. The cross-collateralization clause served this purpose and no other.

If the household furniture that Walker-Thomas previously sold Williams were ordinary property subject to creditor levy, the cross-collateralization clause would be meaningless. If Williams fails to pay for the stereo, Walker-Thomas can reduce its claim to judgment, obtain a writ of execution, and require the sheriff to seize all of Williams's nonexempt assets, including any furniture she owned, regardless of whether she bought it from Walker-Thomas.

A security interest gives a creditor other rights, but they do not matter here. For example, a secured creditor has a right to repossess in the event of a default, but this right can be exercised only if it can be done without a breach of the peace. A breach of the peace includes unauthorized entry into a private home.[27] Hence, the secured creditor's ability to repossess without going to court is relevant when the collateral is a car parked on the street but not when the collateral is household furniture.

Some readers of the case are left with the impression that the cross-collaterization provision functions as a penalty clause, that it gives Walker-Thomas the right to keep all of the property in the event of default independent of how much it is worth. This is wrong. A secured creditor has a right to repossess only to the extent necessary to recover what it is owed and no more. Indeed, as long as the debtor insists, the seller is obliged to sell the property and return any surplus to the debtor.

The function that the cross-collateralization serves, one that the court does not acknowledge or perhaps even understand, makes it easy to justify limits on its enforceability. Given the rationale behind the long-standing legislative policy of putting Williams's household goods beyond the reach of creditors, it makes little sense to allow Walker-Thomas to obtain a waiver of the right in fine print. A waiver of such a right must be done in an environment that allows for reflection and deliberation. If Williams is to give up her right to protect exempt property, she should know that she has the right and that she is giving it up. It is unlikely that Williams would have understood the effect of the clause, even if she read it. If she could not understand it, then it should not be enforced, given the importance the law attaches to exempt property.

One can also take this argument a step further. In a mass market, credit transactions are so routine that it is hard to craft any formal rule that works. The formality must give enough salience to the waiver to ensure that it is made with deliberation. Requiring that a cross-collateralization clause be disclosed conspicuously or made the subject of explicit negotiation is not enough. Explaining the connection between cross-collateralization clauses and exemption laws is not easy even in the law-school classroom. Devising a rule that brings about a fully informed waiver on the floor of an inner-city furniture store is just not possible.

For this reason, it may make sense to ban such clauses altogether. Someone in Williams's position might want to waive her right to exempt property even if she were fully informed. As noted, the household furniture is a good hostage. Her willingness to give up the furniture in the event of default sends a powerful signal that default is unlikely. But we cannot be sure that she will in fact be well informed. If we cannot be sure, we may be better off with an outright ban.[28]

This argument against enforcing some kinds of fine-print terms works because of the connection it makes with another substantive legal policy (our commitment to limit the ability of creditors to reach certain types of assets), not because of vague and abstract notions of bargaining power.

Giving effect to fine print can undercut other substantive policies embedded in the law. Process rights are a case in point. From the beginning, we have always required creditors to cut square corners. If they could not serve their debtors with process and bring them into court, they were out of luck. Such rules can be justified on utilitarian grounds. A court is less likely to make a mistake when both litigants are present. But part of the rationale for these rules is decidedly not utilitarian.

Our conception of limited government requires that, before the state brings force to bear on any citizen, it must follow procedures that respect individual autonomy. Governmental power will not be used against an individual until that individual has notice and a chance to be heard.[29] These rights are not absolute, but the exceptions are narrowly crafted. Many of these rights can be waived, but the waivers must be deliberate.[30]

It is not necessary to find utilitarian justifications for the protections that are part of criminal procedure. Suppose that police and prosecutors did their jobs so well that vanishingly few innocent people were ever brought to trial and that trials were costly and did little to ensure that only the guilty were convicted. We would still insist on a right to a trial. Criminal punishment without due process is barbaric, no matter how efficient.

The procedural hoops through which creditors must jump to invoke the aid of the state rest similarly on both utilitarian and nonutilitarian rationales. The sheriff cannot enter into my home unless I first have a chance to say why he should not. We may not want to leave the waiver of such rights to the forces of competition in the marketplace. Even if the efficient contract would lead to a waiver of the right, our conception of government and individual autonomy might still require that each waiver be a conscious and deliberate act.

The question that needs to be confronted squarely here is how far such arguments should be pressed.[31] Lenders sometimes ask their debtors to waive their right to have a chance to appear in court and dispute their liability on a claim. Creditors want to be able to enforce their claim jumping through as few hoops as possible, but it may make sense to ban such waivers altogether because we do not want to see state force harnessed in such a fashion. Such a waiver is fundamentally different from a warranty disclaimer. Because the use of force by the state is implicated, it is not simply another hidden product attribute.

The law vindicates a number of noninstrumentalist objectives that are not always consistent with individual perceptions of self-interest. Process rights and privacy rights are embedded in the warp and woof of a society. Each decision about the procedures that suit her or the information she is willing to disclose may not lead to the amount of process or privacy that is best for the society as a whole. Boilerplate terms might thus compromise process or privacy values and might be regulated on that account. This rationale, however, does not apply broadly across all types of boilerplate. More to the point, boilerplate is neither where such an inquiry should begin nor where it should end.

Fine Print and Signal Dampening

In a mass marketplace in which there is little dickering or negotiating, legal rules should focus not on discrete transactions but on ensuring the smooth operation of the market as a whole. Much of the law merchant concerned itself with the regulation of the marketplace as a whole. Buyers could keep goods when there was a thief in their chain of title if, but only if, they bought in an open market. Thieves could find no buyers outside the market, because such buyers could not be sure they could keep what they bought, and thieves could not sell inside the market because their open display of stolen goods made it too likely they would be caught. At the same time, buyers who played by the rules were sure to get good title.[32]

As part of making a market work effectively, legal rules should make it easy for buyers to identify different sellers and learn about the attributes of their products. Many legal rules serve this function. The laws of trademark and unfair competition are the most conspicuous examples. These allow a buyer to find a product she likes and tell others about it. Trademark law does nothing to ensure product quality directly, but it works indirectly. With a trademark, sellers with quality products can set themselves apart.

Rules of contract also affect the ability of sellers to set themselves apart. Recall the facts of *Carlill v. Carbolic Smoke Ball Co.*[33] In *Carlill,* the seller ran an advertisement that promised £100 to anyone who used its influenza remedy but nevertheless caught the flu. Carlill used the smoke ball and later caught the flu. When she sued, the seller defended on the ground that the promise was not legally enforceable. The court rejected the company's claim, relying in part on the notion that enforcing such a promise allowed sellers whose products worked to distinguish themselves from sellers whose products did not. Allowing the Carbolic Smoke Ball Companies of this world to escape liability would deprive honest sellers of a way to distinguish themselves. By making such promises enforceable, those with effective cold remedies have an additional way of convincing people that they work.

For our purposes, the aftermath of *Carlill* is the most interesting. After the litigation, the seller ran the same newspaper advertisement and increased the reward to £200, but it added fine print.[34] To be eligible to collect, individuals had to come to the company's offices and sign an application and be subject to the undisclosed conditions set out in the application.[35]

In a circumstance such as this, the seller is using fine print to undercut a representation that is made conspicuously. If fine print is enforced in such circumstances, we are in the same position we would be in if the promise was not enforced at all. The signal sent by the offer of the reward is nullified by the fine print. A buyer in such a world, who reads the reward offer or hears about it, does not take it seriously unless she has also invested the time to read the fine print. Without reading the fine print, she has no way of telling whether the promise means anything. Not only do quacks get away with sham promises, but those with quality goods no longer are able to use the promise of a reward to differentiate themselves from others, at least not without taking the second step of convincing people that fine print does not render the promise meaningless.

Assume that the seller promises to repair its product free of charge if it fails for any reason within five years of purchase. In a world in which fine print is not enforced, a sophisticated buyer could take this language and plug it into the background rules that govern in the absence of explicit agreement. She could evaluate this warranty relative to the price that is being charged and the warranties that competitors are offering. In a world with fine print, it is harder for the seller to make the same promise credibly.

To be sure, the seller cannot deliberately promise one thing in an advertisement and something quite different in the fine print. Rules against fraud prevent this. But even the Carbolic Smoke Ball Company's fine print in its second ad (conditioning the warranty on buyers coming to the company's offices and filling out an application before using the ball) does not directly contradict the promise of the reward. And fine print does not need to be nearly as crude as that language in *Carlill* to alter the conspicuous promise fundamentally. Many other terms can have large effects on the power of the signal that the seller is sending.

Sellers that want to separate themselves from others are not completely powerless. They can make conspicuous promises to the effect that there is no fine print. Such promises ensure that any fine print that does exist will not be effective. But the problem never disappears completely. Warranties sufficiently fine-tuned to be useful cannot be spelled out in a few words of bold type.

A seller's promise to repair free of charge will likely have to be qualified in some degree, such as limitations when the damages to the product stems from the buyer's abuse of it. The power of a warranty, especially one of any complexity, turns in significant measure on forum-selection and choice-of-law provisions. The chosen jurisdiction may measure damages in a different way. It may or may not provide for trial by jury.

It may be more or less convenient for the buyer. The fine print may provide for arbitration of disputes. Arbitration might ensure inexpensive and expert decision making. But it might also steer the litigation toward a forum that will be strongly biased in favor of the seller.

Enforcing fine print makes the entire contract harder to understand. It makes it harder for sellers to set themselves apart from each other. A sensible approach to fine print in this context must account for forces that pull in opposite directions. In a market where search costs are low, fine print allows sellers to customize contract terms to everyone's benefit. By enforcing fine print that most never read, we may be enabling sellers to customize terms and offer a package that is far better than one that imposed only a general obligation to conform to generally recognized norms. If there are enough sophisticated buyers in the marketplace and it is easy enough for them to understand what is in the fine print, the forces of competition will drive sellers toward efficient terms. But there is a dark side here as well. Fine print can limit the ability of sellers to send clear signals. They have to devise ways of assuring buyers that the promise is not being undercut by what is in fine print.

Effective legal rules in this environment should make it easy for buyers to shop. At the same time, they should ensure, or at least not significantly undercut, the ability of sellers to customize their terms. The Magnuson-Moss Warranty Act[36] can be justified using this rationale. A seller of consumer products that uses the word "warranty" commits itself to a number of substantive promises, independent of anything that is said in the fine print.[37] Such a rule has obvious costs, of course. A seller that wishes to make fine-tuned promises with respect to the quality of her goods has more trouble doing so. For example, an efficient warranty might involve a co-payment on the part of the buyer. If she wants to do this, she must conspicuously state that she is offering only a limited warranty.

But the benefits may offset this cost. If a seller uses the word "warranty," buyers know that the seller will repair or replace any defect without cost to them. This right cannot be taken away in fine print. Blocking the operation of fine print makes it cheaper for sellers to distinguish themselves. Similarly, the Uniform Commercial Code makes disclaimers of express warranties ineffective.[38] Every representation that becomes part of the basis of the bargain binds the seller. Moreover, a sophisticated buyer who inspects technical specifications knows that the seller cannot cut back on them in fine print that gives the seller the right to make substitutions or alterations.[39]

One can also argue that limitations on arbitration and forum-selection clauses serve the same purpose. A warranty does no good unless one can be confident that the threat to enforce it is credible. A great warranty enforceable only after arbitration in Nepal is not worth much. If we require any change in the forum-selection, choice-of-law, or arbitration provisions to be conspicuous or put minimum standards in place, we again make it easier for the sophisticated buyer to know that the warranty she sees has teeth.

This rationale for excluding such clauses from the operation of fine print dovetails with the argument that fine print should not undercut substantive policies embedded elsewhere in the law. An arbitration clause can affect the way a sophisticated buyer assesses the explicit representations the seller is making. At the same time, an arbitration clause can undercut process rights that the law regards as particularly important. Some types of arbitration lack many of the features that are fundamental to our notions of process. In the rules of screenwriter arbitration, for example, the litigants do not even know the names of the three arbiters.[40] The arbiters themselves do not meet. Indeed, they do not even know each other's names.[41] Opting in to such an enforcement regime should not be done casually.

For both reasons, it may make sense to require that arbitration or other forum-selection rules be disclosed conspicuously or meet minimum standards. The argument is not that fine print is uniquely subject to abuse as a general matter but rather that among hidden product attributes (including fine print), arbitration is special. The speed of a microprocessor does not undercut any substantive legal policies nor does it dampen any signals in a way that an arbitration clause might.

Fine Print in Perspective

The leading exemplars of the judicial treatment of fine print—*Henningsen* and *Walker-Thomas*—were decided a half century ago. The problems they addressed have long since disappeared. Cartels are unstable, and agreements like the standard warranty in *Henningsen* have a limited life. That agreement collapsed in 1962 when Chrysler, the defendant in *Henningsen,* broke with the others and started to offer its extended powertrain warranty.[42] In today's radically different environment, there is vigorous competition over this product dimension.[43]

The court's rationale in *Walker-Thomas,* one that focused on vague notions of unconscionability, did little to protect those in the position of Williams. More to the point, the particular practice at issue in that case—the cross-collateralization clause—is a dead letter. It was banned outright three decades ago in an uncontroversial regulation issued during the Reagan administration.[44] The problem of protecting Williams today has nothing to do with boilerplate but rather with the best way to regulate the multibillion dollar rent-to-own industry. This business did not even exist at the time of *Walker-Thomas.*[45]

In both *Henningsen* and *Walker-Thomas,* the court's focus on the absence of a dickered bargain blinded it to the aspects of the case that were indeed troublesome. In *Henningsen,* the court did not see that anticompetitive behavior, indeed an outright violation of the Sherman Act, was at work. In *Williams v. Walker-Thomas Furniture,* the court did not seem to understand what cross-collateralization clauses did. That the judges made these errors is explicable. At the time these judges went to law school, Arthur Corbin's and Fritz Kessler's efforts to understand how the law worked in mass markets, as primitive as they seem today, were state of the art.

Corbin and Kessler were among those on whom Justice Francis relies explicitly in his opinion in *Henningsen.*[46] They were still cutting-edge even at the time of the opinion itself and relatively new in the late 1940s when he was in law school. No one can doubt Corbin's and Kessler's place in the pantheon of contract scholars, but we should not neglect the progress made since. The critical insight—the need to look at the effect of legal regulation on markets as a whole—comes in large measure from Alan Schwartz, one of Corbin's successors in the Townsend chair at the Yale Law School. Of course, the contributions of Schwartz and others like him are not the last word either. There is still much about the regulation of markets that we still do not understand. The recent work of Schwartz's own successor in the Townsend chair strongly suggests that we can make use of additional tools, especially those in behavioral economics, as we continue to advance the frontier.[47]

What remains deeply troubling, however, is the extent to which cases as outdated as *Henningsen* and *Williams* continue to define the contours of the debate. In few other fields, even in law, has conventional thought been so fused in amber. Much of the problem is a view of the law that reduces everything to rights that A and B have against each other. From here, it is but a short step to view any troublesome transaction in which there is fine print to be the result of the fine print and the absence of a fully dickered bargain between two equals. The legal challenges that appear from the contracts that evolve in mass markets are often best met by regulating the market as a whole, rather than discrete transactions.

Epilogue

The Boundaries of Contract

Grant Gilmore believed that contract law was dying. A number of cases seemed to be erasing the boundary between contractual liability and noncontractual liability, a development flatly inconsistent with Holmes's notion of contractual obligation being a yes/no, on/off affair. Recall the facts of *Drennan v. Star Paving Co.*[1] A general contractor asks for bids from subcontractors. The general contractor then uses these bids in preparing his own bid. After it is too late for the general contractor to change his bid, the subcontractor learns that he has made a mistake. Can the subcontractor withdraw his bid after it has been relied on? Justice Traynor held that the subcontractor was bound:

> [The subcontractor] had reason not only to expect [the general contractor] to *rely* on its bid but to want him to. Clearly [the subcontractor] had a stake in [the general contractor's] *reliance* on its bid. Given this interest and the fact that [the general contractor] is bound by his own bid, it is only fair that [the general contractor] should have at least an opportunity to accept [the subcontractor's] bid after the general contract has been awarded to him.[2]

Justice Traynor found that the subcontractor should be bound because of the reliance on the part of the general contractor. The promise is at best implied, but the promise itself is not what matters; rather, it is the reliance that arose from the interaction that is important.

Consider a slightly different case. A general contractor wants to know how much to bid on a project. She hires an expert to estimate the cost of construction. The expert comes back with her report. The general

147

contractor relies on the report in making her bid. The contractor wins the contract, but the costs prove to be much higher than the expert predicted and the contractor loses money. Can the general contractor turn around and sue the expert? Our intuition tells us that the expert is not liable, at least if she was not negligent. There is a difference between paying an expert to offer an opinion and getting someone to guarantee that a project will come it at a particular cost.

But there is reliance in this case as well. Traynor's logic applies to the expert as much as it did to the case of the subcontractor. The idea that when people rely on you to their detriment, you should have some obligation to make them whole makes a certain amount of sense, but it does not work everywhere. To get the principle of reliance to work in the hard cases, you have to distinguish the case of the subcontractor from the case of the expert. There are, of course, differences between the subcontractor and the expert, but do these differences have anything to do with reliance? Do they inform our understanding of the basic principles of contract? One can add the qualification that reliance must be "reasonable," but then one faces the challenge of explaining what make some kinds of reliance reasonable and others not. It is not obvious that progress is being made.

Notions that reliance matters and that the boundaries of contract are uncertain tempt us to think problems simpler than they are. Look again at a familiar case—*Goodman v. Dicker.*[3] It is just after World War II. Dicker wants to go into the business of selling radios. Radios after all are the medium of the future. They are great. There are even ventriloquists on the radio. Dicker goes to Goodman. Goodman is in the business of finding potential franchisees for Emerson Radio.

Goodman tells Dicker that he will be given an Emerson franchise. Goodman tells Dicker to hire agents, to start lining up customers, and to be ready for the delivery of radios. Goodman's enthusiasm is understandable. He will get a cut on every radio Dicker sells. Goodman's optimism turns out to be excessive and misleading. Dicker does not get the franchise, and the money he spent preparing to sell the radios is wasted.

The nub of the case is misrepresentation. But the misrepresentation in *Goodman v. Dicker* is not as flagrant as in the usual case of fraud. In the typical fraud case, the person makes outright lies from which he profits directly. In this case, Goodman stood to gain only indirectly by the efforts of Dicker. None of the money Dicker spends ends up in Goodman's hands or even Emerson's. Goodman profits only if everything he said turned out to be true.

The traditional misrepresentation action may or may not be available under these facts. We must confront this question directly. The language of promissory estoppel and reliance are neither implicated nor useful. We should focus squarely on the question of whether this plaintiff should be able to take advantage of a long-established tort action, not whether the boundaries of contract should be modified.

Efforts to reconceive the boundaries of contract grew out of unhappiness with the articulation of basic principles at the end of the nineteenth century. This formalization of contract doctrine did less than their partisans claimed. Principles such as bargained-for consideration were too malleable. *De Cicco v. Schweitzer* illustrates.[4] Justice Cardozo confronted a father who promised to give his daughter and the count to whom she was engaged $2,500 a year after they married. Cardozo found the father's promise supported by consideration. Where was the consideration? What detriment did the daughter and the count incur in exchange for the promise? Cardozo pointed out that, even though neither was legally bound to go through with the marriage at the time of the promise, they did anyway. One suspects Cardozo found consideration because he thought that enforcing a promise here was a good idea. Perhaps it is. One may need to give minor European nobility a legally enforceable right in such situations. Henry James suggests as much. But in the hands of Cardozo, the doctrine of consideration is too soft. Its virtues as a formal rule disappear if consideration can be found any time a judge wants to enforce a promise.

The logic of the bargained-for exchange also leads in directions that at times seem to make little sense. When nineteenth-century doctrinalists tried to play out the logic of the bargained-for exchange, they quickly looked ridiculous. The classic is the Brooklyn Bridge problem. I promise you $100 if you walk across the Brooklyn Bridge. Once you cross it, I am obliged to pay you. But what if I revoke my promise just as you are almost across? Until you have crossed, you have not given me or promised to give me what I have asked for. There is, as yet, no bargained-for exchange. Hence, I am free to revoke. To hold otherwise would be to enforce a unilateral promise. It is like one hand clapping. The result was hard on you, but you needed this result to preserve symmetry.

Once you go down this road, it is hard to find your way. Why should we care about symmetry? If I want to commit myself to making an offer and not revoking it, why should I not be able to do it? Rigorous logic, relentlessly and mercilessly applied to a legal problem, swiftly decays into nonsense.

There was a belief in the late part of the nineteenth century, inspired by Langdell, that law was a science. There were principles in the great beyond that were fixed and immutable. A court sitting on Mars would apply the same principles. We should not be surprised that such fantasies created trouble.

The embrace of reliance and promissory estoppel was a reaction against expecting formal legal rules to bear more weight than was reasonable. But Corbin and his contemporaries were unaware of the subtle vices of their own approach. Although they did not believe that legal rules were immutable, they believed that legal rules could be divined from widely shared norms of behavior. Although these norms provide insights, they cannot illuminate everything. Hard cases do not have easy answers.

Defenders of both the classical doctrine like bargained-for consideration and modern notions of reliance too often failed to confront the limitations embedded in any law of contracts. The test of a formal rule should not be some inner logic but rather the way it channels behavior. And merely because we believe people should, as a moral matter, keep serious promises reasonably relied on does not mean that the state, with its imperfect mechanisms to enforce these promises, should always stand at the ready to do so.

Clear rules that let parties know where they stand are useful even if they are not eternal truths. The norms and expectations of those who adhere to principles of fair dealing, even if they are far from being identical to the law, provide a useful way to assess the obligations that parties to a contract have taken on themselves. But appreciating these principles requires understanding their limits.

Even if the tools we use to map the world are imperfect, we can make progress in understanding the law of contracts and the way that it facilitates mutually beneficial bargains. Economics has heavily influenced the contemporary understanding of contract, but it is better at providing a method for organizing our thinking than at generating predictions about the exact shape that the law does or should take. Other generations will undoubtedly use different tools to make further progress. As Ronald Coase observed long ago, problems of welfare economics must ultimately dissolve into a study of aesthetics and morals.[5]

Regardless of the tools that we use, we cannot expect pat answers. The law of contracts and the world in which it operates are both too rich and too subtle to be reduced to a single metric. We must continue to reconstruct the law of contracts, remembering that the test of new organizing ideas or formal rules is whether they are useful. They will be man-made rather than God-given. The principles we fashion cannot be independent of time and place. As Aristotle reminds us, fires burn here as in Persia, but the laws are different.[6]

NOTES

Introduction

1. The novelist in question was one of the best known of the day and Holmes's own father. See Oliver Wendell Holmes, Sr., *The Poet at the Breakfast-Table* (Osgood 1872).

2. Oliver Wendell Holmes, Jr., *The Common Law* 2 (Little, Brown 1881).

3. See id. at 35.

4. Grant Gilmore, *The Death of Contract* 102 (Ohio State University Press 1974).

5. These facts are loosely based on Embry v. Hargadine-McKittrick Dry Goods Co., 127 Mo. App. 383, 105 S.W. 777 (1907).

6. Globe Refining Co. v. Landa Cotton Oil Co., 190 U.S. 540 (1903).

1. Objective Intent

1. The contemporary understanding of the case—which is the one presented here—is due to the work of the great legal historian Brian Simpson. See A. W. Brian Simpson, "Contracts for Cotton to Arrive: The Case of Two Ships *Peerless*," 11 *Cardozo L. Rev.* 287 (1989). I follow his account closely.

2. Grant Gilmore, The Death of Contract 37 (Ohio State University Press 1974).

3. Savigny is quoted in T. E. Holland, *The Elements of Jurisprudence*, 2nd ed. (Oxford, Clarendon Press, 1882), 194.

4. See Marlow Ediger & D. Bhaskara Rao, *Philosophy and Curriculum* 56 (Discovery Publg. 2003).

5. Holmes, *The Common Law*, at 309.

6. Gilmore, *The Death of Contract*, at 41.

7. Holmes, *The Common Law*, at 309–10.

8. Hotchkiss v. National City Bank, 200 F. 287, 293 (S.D.N.Y. 1911).

9. See Judah P. Benjamin, *A Treatise on the Law of Sale of Personal Property; Reference to the American Decisions and to the French Code and Civil Law* 347–48 (J. Perkins ed., first American edition 1875). Simpson's discussion of Benjamin can be found in Simpson, "Contracts for Cotton to Arrive," at 329–30.

10. At least, if one accepts, as I do, Simpson's reconstruction of the facts.

11. This again assumes that Simpson's reconstruction is accurate.

12. Frigaliment Importing Co. v. B.N.S. International Sales Corp., 190 F. Supp. 116 (S.D.N.Y. 1960).

13. See Flower City Painting Contractors v. Gumina Construction Co., 591 F.2d 162 (2d Cir. 1979).

14. United Rentals, Inc. v. RAM Holdings, Inc., 937 A.2d 810 (Del. Ch. 2007).

15. Lisa Bernstein has done the foundational work here. See, e.g., Lisa Bernstein, "Merchant Law in a Merchant Court: Rethinking the Code's Search for Immanent Business Norms," 144 *U. Pa. L. Rev.* 1765 (1996).

2. The Bargained-for Exchange

1. 124 N.Y. 538, 27 N.E. 256 (1891). The following discussion draws from a lecture I gave in 1992; see Douglas G. Baird, "Reconstructing Contracts" (Katz Lecture 1992), Chicago John M. Olin Law and Economics Working Paper No. 11 (2d Series). I elaborated further in Douglas G. Baird, "Reconstructing Contracts: *Hamer v. Sidway*," in *Contract Stories* 160–85 (Foundation Press 2007).

2. Pinnel's Case, 5 Coke Rep. 117a (1602).

3. O. W. Holmes, Jr., *The Common Law* 293–94 (Little, Brown 1881).

4. 11 N.Y.S. 182 (Sup. Ct. 1890).

5. 4 *Harv. L. Rev.* 237. The note appeared in the December 1890 issue of the *Harvard Law Review,* an issue that also included Warren and Brandeis's landmark article on the right to privacy. See Samuel D. Warren & Louis D. Brandeis, "The Right to Privacy," 4 *Harv. L. Rev.* 193 (1890).

6. 124 N.Y. at 546.

7. Trial record at 93, Hamer v. Sidway, 124 N.Y. 538, 27 N.E. 256 (1891) [hereinafter "Record"].

8. Record at 94.

9. Millard v. Clark, 27 N.Y.S. 631 (1894).

10. Record at 56.

11. Record at 58–59.

12. See Seavey v. Drake, 62 N.H. 393 (1882).

13. See Ricketts v. Scothorn, 77 N.W. 365 (Neb. 1898).

14. See Hendrik Hartog, "Someday All This Will Be Yours: Inheritance, Adoption, and Obligation in Capitalist America," 79 *Ind. L.J.* 345 (2004).

15. See Grant Gilmore, *The Death of Contract* 62–65 (Ohio State University Press 1974).

16. Arthur L. Corbin, "Does a Pre-Existing Duty Defeat Consideration?—Recent Noteworthy Decisions," 27 *Yale L.J.* 362, 376 (1917).

17. See Alan Schwartz & Robert E. Scott, "Precontractual Liability," 120 *Harv. L. Rev.* 661 (2007).

18. Allegheny College v. National Chautauqua County Bank, 246 N.Y. 369, 159 N.E. 173 (1927).

19. 20 Mass. (3 Pick.) 207 (1825).

20. The definitive investigation into the historical record can be found in Geoffrey R. Watson, "In the Tribunal of Conscience: *Mills v. Wyman* Reconsidered," 71 *Tulane L. Rev.* 1749 (1997). Geoffrey Watson, the careful historian, resists retelling the story from any single point of view and would likely caution that the one set out in the text is only one of a number of possible narratives that can be reconstructed from the record. Anyone wishing to understand this case must begin with Watson's article.

21. See Watson, "In the Tribunal of Conscience," at 1759.

22. Id. at 1761 n.72.

23. See http://freenet.buffalo.edu/bah/h/sidway/index.html#Franklin8.

24. See Sidway v. Cuba State Bank, 68 Sickels 634, 20 N.E. 878 (N.Y. 1889).

25. Willie returned the original to his uncle at his uncle's request many years before, but it was not found among the uncle's effects until later. See Record at 35.

26. Record at 51–52.

27. Hamer's lawyer tried to downplay the significance of the fact that the amount equaled exactly what William promised Willie by arguing that only half the loan was to Willie. The other half was to Willie's father, Willie's partner in the business.

28. Record at 72.

29. Willie goes so far as to say that he never made any assignment of his rights against William to Louise. Record at 51. Like other parts of his story, Willie's assertion is not credible. Willie's father testifies to the contrary, Record at 40, as does his own lawyer. (The lawyer filed an affidavit stating that he "saw an assignment in writing, made by William E. Story 2d, of this claim to the plaintiff." Record at 95. The affidavit was intended to help Willie and his family, as it was their effort to explain the error in the original complaint.) It may be that Willie made a general assignment of any rights he might have against the uncle at a time when he did not know whether his uncle might have left some modest bequest to him.

We do not know that much about the firm of Swift and Weaver, the lawyers that Willie and his family used for many years (in its various incarnations). It had its own share of problems at the time. One of the associates in the firm, indeed the one who notarized the lawyer's unusual affidavit, committed suicide just a few days after the trial ended. See "Probable Suicide at Buffalo," *New York Times,* July 29, 1889, at 1. The timing is an odd coincidence, but there is no other reason to think it connected with this case. Only for the mystery writer with a historical-legal bent does it present another possible narrative.

30. See 14 Stat. 531–32, 534, 39th Cong., Sess. II, ch. 176, §29, §35 (1867). For the parallel provisions under current law, see 11 U.S.C. §548, §727.

31. Willie says he asked his lawyers whether, to make the assignment effective, his wife had to give him an actual dollar or whether it was sufficient to allege it in the written assignment. See Record at 52.

32. Record at 37.

33. I am inferring Sidway's frustration and refusal to believe Willie and his relatives from that of his lawyers. It becomes manifest at various points during the trial, especially when Willie and his father contradict each other or say things that are especially implausible.

34. See Gary Lawson, "Proving the Law," 86 Nw. U. L. Rev. 859 (1992).

35. Record at 45 ("They never had any words that I know of. I have never in my life know them to have a word").

36. Willie, however, was disappointed that "he was left out in the cold" and those close in his circle did express their "astonishment" at what others had received. Record at 60.

37. See "Death of William E. Storey [sic]," Buffalo Daily Courier, Jan. 30, 1887, at 4.

38. Record at 37–38.

39. See Record at 40.

40. Record at 89.

41. Record at 89.

42. Record at 90.

43. Record at 44 ("that was the first house that we fixed over").

44. Putting all the rights against William into Louise's hands was something that someone wanted done quickly. When Willie returned from the funeral, he stopped in Elmira only long enough to meet his wife and her mother at the train station and oversee his wife executing the assignment of her rights against William (consisting only of the promise Willie had assigned to her) to her mother. Willie presumably brought back from Buffalo documents that the family lawyers had prepared there.

45. Cass Sunstein explores these in the environment of a collegial court, where incompletely reasoned agreements are the norm. See Cass R. Sunstein, One Case at a Time (1999). The costs of having a "completely reasoned" account are, of course, somewhat different in this environment, as they include the psychic costs of unpacking and monetizing understandings between blood relatives.

46. See Hartog, "Someday All This Will Be Yours."

3. Holmes's Bad Man

1. The germ of this chapter originated in an essay for a Festschrift in honor of Richard Epstein. See Douglas G. Baird, "The Holmesian Bad Man's First Critic," 44 Tulsa L. Rev. 739 (2009). For an excellent account of the events

leading to the writing of "The Path of the Law," see David J. Seipp, "Holmes's Path," 77 *B.U. L. Rev.* 515 (1997).

2. Oliver Wendell Holmes, Jr., "The Path of the Law," 10 *Harv. L. Rev.* 457, 459 (1897).

3. See Mark DeWolfe Howe, *Justice Oliver Wendell Holmes: The Proving Years, 1870–1882* vol. 2, 5–8 (1963).

4. Id. at 7.

5. One of the most effective of these attacks on Holmes was the one launched by one of my teachers in law school, Yosal Rogat. For his views of Holmes as the Young Astronomer, see Yosal Rogat, "The Judge as Spectator," 31 *U. Chi. L. Rev.* 213, 243–56 (1964).

6. Buck v. Bell, 274 U.S. 200, 207 (1927).

7. Holmes, "The Path of the Law," at 462.

8. The conspicuous exception is Seipp, "Holmes's Path." This debate surfaces only briefly in "Path of the Law," with Holmes observing merely that "Mr. Harriman in his very able little book upon Contracts has been misled." Holmes, "The Path of the Law," at 462.

9. Harriman's critique of Holmes recalls the young Richard Epstein's critique of Richard Posner. It also connects with Richard Epstein's work on tortious interference with contract. See Richard A. Epstein, "Inducement of Breach of Contract as a Problem of Ostensible Ownership," 16 *J. Leg. Stud.* 1 (1987).

10. Edward Avery Harriman, "The Nature of Contractual Obligation," 4 *Nw. L. Rev.* 97 (1896).

11. Id. at 99.

12. Id. at 100.

13. Id. at 108.

14. See Holmes, "The Path of the Law," at 462.

15. Seipp, "Holmes's Path," at 527 (Ltr. from Oliver Wendell Holmes, Jr., to Edward Avery Harriman (Jan. 7, 1896)).

16. See Paul R. Thagard, "The Best Explanation: Criteria for Theory Choice," 75 *J. Phil.* 76, 87–89 (1978).

17. For a formal exposition of this idea, see id. at 87–89.

18. See Edward Avery Harriman, *The Law of Contracts* 322 (2d ed., Little, Brown & Co. 1901).

19. Id. at 322.

20. Id.

21. Holmes tried to explain this distinction in two letters to Pollock. He emphasized that his focus was on the way in which a discrete act triggered the legal obligation, not that the person was promising either to perform or pay damages. See *The Pollock–Holmes Letters: The Correspondence of Mr. Justice Holmes and Sir Frederick Pollock, 1874–1932,* at 177–78, 233–34 (Mark De-Wolfe Howe ed. 1942). Others, of course, have made this basic point that Holmes

was trying to provide a description of the law rather than denying its moral content. See, e.g., Joseph M. Perillo, "Misreading Oliver Wendell Holmes on Efficient Breach and Tortious Interference," 68 *Fordham L. Rev.* 1085 (2000).

22. To put the point formally, even if his theory was somewhat more complex, it possessed greater "concilience" than Holmes's. See Thagard, "The Best Explanation," at 79–85.

23. Holmes, "The Path of the Law," at 462–63.

24. Id.

25. Harriman, *The Law of Contracts,* at 322 (quoting Pollock & Maitland, *History of English Law,* vol. 2, 593).

26. 15 S.W. 844 (Mo. 1891).

27. Id. at 848.

28. Lord Mansfield sets out this idea of the presumptive interdependence of promises in Kingston v. Preston, 2 Doug. 689 (K.B. 1773).

29. Harriman, *The Law of Contracts,* at 323.

30. Lumley v. Gye, 118 Eng. Rep. 749 (1853).

31. Of course, others have noticed that Holmes's account of contract law does not mesh well with tortious interference. My principal point here is that Harriman's does.

32. See Harris v. Perl, 197 A.2d 359, 363 (N.J. 1963).

33. See Fred S. McChesney, "Tortious Interference with Contract versus 'Efficient' Breach: Theory and Empirical Evidence," 28 *J. Leg. Stud.* 131, 168–69 (1999).

34. Id. at 169–70.

35. See Epstein, "Inducement of Breach of Contract as a Problem of Ostensible Ownership."

36. Harriman, *The Law of Contracts,* at 322 (quoting Pollock & Maitland, *History of English Law* vol. 2, 593).

37. The evidence suggests that after litigation in which parties obtain specific relief, parties do not bargain with each other, even when such bargains might be mutually beneficial. See Ward Farnsworth, "Do Parties to Nuisance Cases Bargain after Judgment?: A Glimpse inside the Cathedral," 66 *U. Chi. L. Rev.* 373 (1999).

38. This was one of the favorite axioms of my late colleague Walter Blum.

4. The Expectation Damages Principle and Its Limits

1. See Richard A. Posner, "A Theory of Negligence," 1 *J. Leg. Stud.* 29 (1972).

2. Grant Gilmore, *The Death of Contract* 103 (Ohio State University Press 1974).

3. The discussion that follows draws from Douglas G. Baird, "The Law and Economics of Contract Damages," in *Chicago Lectures in Law and Economics* (Foundation Press 2000).

4. Id. at §4.8.

5. Richard A. Posner, *Economic Analysis of Law* §4.8 (5th ed., Aspen Publishers 1997).

6. See id.

7. 8 F. 463 (W.D. Pa. 1881).

8. The first comprehensive treatment of this question is Thomas H. Jackson, "'Anticipatory Repudiation' and the Temporal Element in Contract Law: An Economic Inquiry into Contract Damages in Cases of Prospective Nonperformance," 31 *Stan. L. Rev.* 69 (1978). My discussion follows Jackson closely. For a critique, see Alan Schwartz & Robert Scott, *Commercial Transactions: Principles and Policies* 323–25 (1982).

9. Of course, expectation damages are not, in practice, completely compensatory. In practice, a hotel owner cares about her reputation and would not be indifferent to canceling the convention. I am abstracting from such uncompensated harms here to underscore the dark side to expectation damages.

10. Steven Shavell was the first to make this important insight. Steven Shavell, "Damage Measures for Breach of Contract," 11 *Bell J. Econ.* 466 (1980).

11. For background to this case, see Richard Danzig, "*Hadley v. Baxendale*: A Story in the Industrialization of Law," 4 *J. Legal Stud.* 249 (1975).

12. Hypotheticals tend to be handed down from one law professor to another. Bob Gordon gave me this "hop-in-buddy" hypothetical when we were both teaching contracts together at Stanford.

13. This second line of reasoning, arguing that a "penalty default" should apply to high-damage types, begins with important work by Ian Ayres and Robert Gertner. See Ian Ayres & Robert Gertner, "Filling Gaps in Incomplete Contracts: An Economic Theory of Default Rules," 99 *Yale L.J.* 87 (1989). For a critique of their work, see Jason Johnston, "Strategic Bargaining and the Economic Theory of Contract Default Rules," 100 *Yale L.J.* 615 (1990).

14. It is worth noting, however, that one of the minority jurisdictions that appears to accept the *Globe Refining* test is New York. See Kenford Co., Inc. v. County of Erie, 73 N.Y.2d 312, 537 N.E.2d 176, 540 N.Y.S.2d 1 (1989); Bi-Economy Market, Inc. v. Harleysville Ins. Co. of New York, 10 N.Y.3d 187, 886 N.E.2d 127, 856 N.Y.S.2d 505 (2008). Many contracts, especially ones involving large corporate transactions, turn on New York law.

15. See Richard Craswell, "Contract Remedies, Renegotiation, and the Theory of Efficient Breach," 61 *S. Cal. L. Rev.* 629 (1988).

16. These facts are drawn from Muldoon v. Lynch, 6 P. 417 (1885).

5. Terms of Engagement

1. The background to *Swift v. Tysen* is set out in T. Freyer, *Harmony and Dissonance: The* Swift *and* Erie *Cases in American Federalism* 17–43 (New York University Press 1981).

2. The harder question for him was whether, in addition to acting in good faith, Swift gave value when he canceled the antecedent debt. This part of the opinion remains good law, even though the relevant source of substantive law is now the *Uniform Commercial Code,* rather than general federal common law. See Swift v. Tyson, 41 U.S. 1 (1842). The opinion itself, in addition to misspelling Tysen's name, focuses largely on a procedural issue.

3. See Karl N. Llewellyn, *The Common Law Tradition: Deciding Appeals* 410–21 (1960)

4. See In re Manhattan Investment Fund Ltd., 397 Bankr. 1 (S.D.N.Y. 2007).

5. An excellent overview of the law here can be found in Mark A. McDermott, "Ponzi Schemes and the Law of Fraudulent and Preferential Transfers," 72 *Am. Bankr. L.J.* 157 (1998).

6. See Hayes v. Palm Seedlings Partners-A, 916 F.2d 528, 536 (9th Cir. 1990) ("if the circumstances would place a reasonable person on inquiry of a debtor's fraudulent purpose, and a diligent inquiry would have discovered the fraudulent purpose, then the transfer is fraudulent"); Jobin v. McKay, 84 F.3d 1330, 1338 (10th Cir. 1996); Bonded Financial Services, Inc. v. European American Bank, 838 F.2d 890, 897–98 (7th Cir. 1988) ("recipient of a voidable transfer may lack good faith if he possessed enough knowledge of the events to induce a reasonable person to investigate").

7. See McDermott, "Ponzi Schemes and the Law of Fraudulent and Preferential Transfers," at 178.

8. As Judge Posner has noted, "only a very foolish, very naive, very greedy, or very Machiavellian investor would jump at a chance to obtain a return on his passive investment of 10 to 20 percent a month." See Scholes v. Lehmann, 56 F.3d 750, 760 (7th Cir. 1995).

9. See Neil Behrmann, "Bear Stearns Wins Appeal against Investors Seeking Recovery of Manhattan Fund Losses," *Infovest21 News,* July 1, 2008.

10. See Anthony Kronman, "Mistake, Disclosure, Information and the Law of Contracts," 7 *J. Legal Stud.* 1 (1978).

11. 15 U.S. 178, 194 (1817).

12. See generally Chi. Bd. of Trade, Chicago Board of Trade Rulebook, available at http://www.cmegroup.com/rulebook/cbot-rulebook-listing.html. Disclosure of positions is typically to the board itself, not to other traders.

13. Henry G. Manne, *Insider Trading and the Stock Market* 159, 165–66 (Free Press 1966).

14. For illustrations of competing views on disclosure rules, see Frank H. Easterbrook & Daniel R. Fischel, "Mandatory Disclosure and the Protection of Investors," 70 *Va. L. Rev.* 669 (1984); and John C. Coffee, Jr., "Market Failure and the Economic Case for a Mandatory Disclosure System," 70 *Va. L. Rev.* 717 (1984).

15. The facts in this illustration are based on SEC v. Texas Gulf Sulphur Co., 401 F.2d 833 (2d Cir. 1968).

16. See Harris v. Tyson, 24 Pa. 347, 359 (1855) ("A person who knows that there is a mine on the land of another may nevertheless buy it").

17. See Texas Gulf Sulphur Co., 401 F.2d at 847–49, 851–52. The different treatment arises by virtue of Rule 10b-5 of the Securities Exchange Act of 1934. 17 C.F.R. §240.10b-5 (2008).

18. See Kronman, "Mistake, Disclosure, Information and the Law of Contracts."

19. See Ronald J. Gilson & Reinier H. Kraakman, "The Mechanisms of Market Efficiency," 70 *Va. L. Rev.* 549, 565–79 (1984).

20. See, e.g., Manne, *Insider Trading and the Stock Market,* at 159, 165–66.

21. See Ruben Lee, *What Is an Exchange: The Automation, Management, and Regulation of Financial Markets* 247 (Oxford University Press 1998).

22. Restatement (Second) of Torts §551.

23. See Restatement (Second) of Contracts §161(b).

24. Los Angeles Unified School Dist. v. Great American Ins. Co., 234 P.3d 490 (Cal. 2010).

25. Dyke v. Zaiser, 182 P.2d 344 (Cal. App. 1947).

26. Jappe v. Mandt, 278 P.2d 940 (Cal. App. 1955).

27. See Kim Lane Scheppelle, *Legal Secrets: Equality and Efficiency in the Common Law* 269–98 (University of Chicago Press 1988).

28. 15 U.S. at 190.

29. This aspect of the case is set out in Joshua Kaye, "Disclosure, Information, the Law of Contracts, and the Mistaken Use of *Laidlaw v. Organ,*" 79 *Mississippi L.J.* 577 (2010).

30. 941 F.2d 588 (7th Cir. 1991).

31. See Todd Rakoff, "Good Faith in Contract Performance: *Market Street Associates Ltd. Partnership v. Frey,*" 120 *Harv. L. Rev.* 1187 (2007).

32. Courts are split on whether these contracts are valid waivers of claims under the securities laws. Compare Harsco Corp v. Segui, 91 F.3d 337, 341–48 (2d Cir. 1996) (upholding contract and dismissing claim), with AES Corp. v. Dow Chemical Co., 325 F.3d 174, 180 (3d Cir. 2003) (refusing to hold as a matter of law that nonreliance provisions are sufficient to immunize any Rule 10b-5 claims).

33. See Daniel Sullivan, "Comment, Big Boys and Chinese Walls," 75 *U. Chi. L. Rev.* 533 (2008).

6. Mistake, Excuse, and Implicit Terms

1. If I sell you goods knowing them to be defective, you do not need to have a warranty in order for you to be able to recover from me.

2. This argument is developed in Janet Kiholm Smith & Richard Smith, "Contract Law, Mutual Mistake, and Incentives to Produce and Disclose Information," 19 *J. Legal Stud.* 467 (1990).

3. Jackson v. Seymour, 71 S.E.2d 181 (Va. 1952).

4. For a discussion of this problem, see Andrew Kull, "Unilateral Mistake: The Baseball Card Case," 70 *Wash. U. L. Quarterly* 57 (1992).

5. Elsinore Union Elementary School District v. Kastorff, 353 P.2d 713 (Cal. 1960).

6. Opera Co. of Boston, Inc. v. Wolf Trap Foundation for Performing Arts, 817 F.2d 1094 (4th Cir. 1987).

7. "Martinelli Seized by Illness in 'Aida': Tenor Suffers Attack of Acute Indigestion as He Sings 'Celeste' Aria," *New York Times,* Feb. 27, 1938, p. 1.

8. 817 F.2d at 1102.

9. 817 F.2d at 1103.

10. See Andrew Kull, "Mistake, Frustration, and the Windfall Principle of Contract Remedies," 43 *Hastings L.J.* 1 (1992).

11. Id.

12. Fibrosa Spolka Akcyjna v. Fairbairn L.C.B. Ltd., [1943] A.C. 32.

13. 6 & 7 Geo. VI, c. 40.

14. 164 P. 143 (Kansas 1917).

15. Albre Marble & Tile Co. v. John Bowen Co., 155 N.E.2d 437 (Mass. 1959).

16. See Victor P. Goldberg, "Impossibility and Related Excuses," 144 *J. Institutional & Theoretical Econ.* 100, 104–5 (1988).

7. Duress and the Availability of the Legal Remedy

1. This discussion draws on an essay written in honor of Richard Posner's first twenty-five years on the federal bench. See Douglas G. Baird, "The Young Astronomers," 74 *U. Chi. L. Rev.* 1641 (2007).

2. See, e.g., Levine v. Blumenthal, 186 A. 457, 458 (1936) ("The principle is firmly imbedded in our jurisprudence that a promise to do what the promisor is already legally bound to do is an unreal consideration").

3. See Austin Instrument, Inc. v. Loral Corp., 29 N.Y.2d 124, 272 N.E.2d 533, 534 (1971).

4. Selmer Co. v. Blakeslee-Midwest Co., 704 F.2d 924, 927 (7th Cir. 1983) (Posner, J.).

5. 127 F.3d 574 (7th Cir. 1997).

6. 117 F. 99 (9th Cir. 1902).

7. *Alaska Packers'* has been cited thirteen times in the last quarter century. Twelve of those citations appeared in cases decided by the Seventh Circuit, of which Posner authored eight. Of the other four, three were authored by the other great judge-scholar of our time, Frank Easterbrook.

8. Selmer, 704 F.2d at 927.

9. Professional Service Network, Inc v. American Alliance Holding Co, 238 F.3d 897, 900 (7th Cir. 2001) (Posner).

10. Debora Threedy has made a comprehensive study of the record in the case that bears this point out. Debora L. Threedy, "A Fish Story: *Alaska Packers' Association v. Domenico,*" in Douglas G. Baird, ed., *Contracts Stories* 335, 342 (Foundation 2006). For the full trial transcript of the case, see Transcript of Record, *Alaska Packers' Assocation v. Domenico,* No. 789, 18–22 (9th Cir. filed Feb. 4, 1902), available at http://old.law.utah.edu/faculty/bios/threedyd/three-dyd_alaska_transcript.pdf.

11. 127 F.3d at 579.

12. Id.

13. Id.

14. See, e.g., Trompler, Inc. v. NLRB, 338 F.3d 747, 751 (7th Cir. 2003) ("Seamen on board a ship that was fishing for salmon in Alaskan waters during the short fishing season struck for higher wages. The captain agreed to modify the workers' employment contract to pay them the higher wages they were demanding").

15. Posner wrote *Oxxford* at the time he was chief judge of the Seventh Circuit and more interested than usual in problems of judicial administration.

16. This standard way of thinking about preliminary injunctions as a way of minimizing Type I and Type II error is, of course, another contribution of Posner's. See American Hospital Supply Corp v. Hospital Products Ltd, 780 F.2d 589 (7th Cir. 1986).

17. See Kolz v. Greer, 1995 WL 231845 (7th Cir.) Posner was the chief judge of the Seventh Circuit from 1993 through 2000.

18. 226 F.3d 535 (7th Cir. 2000).

19. 29 N.Y.2d 124, 272 N.E.2d 533 (1971).

8. Fine Print

1. The discussion in this chapter draws on two essays first presented at conferences at the University of Michigan. See Douglas G. Baird, "The Boilerplate Puzzle," 104 *Mich. L. Rev.* 933 (2006); Douglas G. Baird, "Commercial Norms and the Fine Art of the Small Con," 98 *Mich. L. Rev.* 2716 (2000).

2. See, e.g., N.Y. Gen. Bus. Law §350-a (McKinney 2004).

3. See Creola Johnson, "Payday Loans: Shrewd Business or Predatory Lending?," 87 *Minn. L. Rev.* 1 (2002).

4. See, e.g., Federal Trade Commission Regulations for Door-to-Door Sales, 16 C.F.R. §429.

5. Donald R. Katz, The Big Store: Inside the Crisis and Revolution at Sears 9–10 (1987).

6. 32 N.J. 358, 161 A.2d 69 (1960).

7. 350 F.2d 445 (D.C. Cir. 1965).

8. See Douglas Brinkley, Wheels for the World: Henry Ford, His Company, and a Century of Progress 1903–2003, at 181–82 (2003).

9. Again, this idea has been well known for a long time. See, e.g., Douglas G. Baird & Robert Weisberg, Rules, Standards, and the Battle of the Forms: A Reassessment of §2-207, 68 Va. L. Rev. 1217, 1253–55 (1982); Victor P. Goldberg, The "Battle of the Forms": Fairness, Efficiency, and the Best-Shot Rule, 76 Or. L. Rev. 155 (1997); Alan Schwartz & Louis L. Wilde, Intervening in Markets on the Basis of Imperfect Information: A Legal and Economic Analysis, 127 U. Pa. L. Rev. 630, 636–39 (1979).

10. See David W. Maurer, *The Big Con: The Story of the Confidence Man and the Confidence Game* 248–77 (Random House 1940).

11. Id. at 157.

12. 161 A.2d 69 (N.J. 1960).

13. Id. at 75.

14. Id. at 95.

15. Id. at 87.

16. Id. at 86.

17. Id. at 87.

18. The idea that the activities of trade associations raise antitrust concerns goes back for decades. See, e.g., Maple Flooring Mfrs. Ass'n v. United States, 268 U.S. 563 (1925); Am. Column & Lumber Co. v. United States, 257 U.S. 377 (1921).

19. For a discussion of how warranties serve this function, see Sanford J. Grossman, "The Informational Role of Warranties and Private Disclosure about Product Quality," 24 *J.L. & Econ.* 461 (1981).

20. See Fed. Trade Comm'n, Report on the Motor Vehicle Industry at 56–57 (1939).

21. See George L. Priest, "A Theory of the Consumer Product Warranty," 90 *Yale L.J.* 1297 (1981).

22. See Amos Tversky & Daniel Kahneman, "Judgment under Uncertainty: Heuristics and Biases," 185 *Science* 1124, 1129 (1974). Russell Korobkin provides an excellent overview of behavioral economics and standard form contracts in Russell Korobkin, "Bounded Rationality, Standard Form Contracts, and Unconscionability," 70 *U. Chi. L. Rev.* 1203 (2003). The approach offered here differs importantly from Korobkin's in two ways. First, it uses principles already embedded in the law (such as the rules governing exempt property and concerns about due process) to identify those terms we need to worry most about when consumers are boundedly rational. Second, it explicitly considers the extent to which the legal enforcement of standard terms should embrace nonutilitarian objectives.

23. See Robert E. Scott, "A Relational Theory of Secured Financing," 86 *Colum. L. Rev.* 901, 930 (1986).

24. See Lon L. Fuller, "Consideration and Form," 41 *Colum. L. Rev.* 799, 800 (1941).

25. Taking a nonpossessory, nonpurchase money security interest in a wedding ring and other household goods is an unfair credit practice. See FTC Unfair Credit Practices Rules, 16 C.F.R. §§444.1(i), 444.2(a)(4). Apart from purchase money security interests, such security interest is voidable under 11 U.S.C. §522(f)(1)(B), (f)(4)(A)(xiv). The exception for purchase money security interests is based on the idea that the loan enables the debtor to acquire the property in the first instance.

26. 350 F.2d 445 (D.C. Cir. 1965).

27. See U.C.C. §9-609(b)(2); James J. White & Robert S. Summers, *Uniform Commercial Code* 4:385–86 (5th ed. 2002).

28. Sunstein and others have unpacked the idea of paternalism in this fashion, distinguishing between ensuring deliberate choice ("weak paternalism") and limiting choices altogether ("strong paternalism"). See Cass R. Sunstein, "Boundedly Rational Borrowing," 73 *U. Chi. L. Rev.* 249 (2006).

29. The use of state force is precisely what animates Fuentes v. Shevin, 407 U.S. 67 (1972).

30. The idea that waivers of such things as the right to counsel must be deliberate is the dominant theme of the Supreme Court's criminal procedure jurisprudence. See, e.g., Von Moltke v. Gillies, 332 U.S. 708, 724 (1948).

31. Margaret Jane Radin, "Humans, Computers, and Binding Commitment," 75 *Ind. L.J.* 1125, 1161 (2000).

32. See Saul Levmore, "Variety and Uniformity in the Treatment of the Good-Faith Purchaser," 16 *J. Legal Stud.* 43 (1987).

33. (1893) 1 Q.B. 256 (U.K.).

34. As with *Raffles v. Wichelhaus*, Brian Simpson was the first person to understand what was in fact going on in this case. See A. W. B. Simpson, "Quackery and Contract Law: The Case of the Carbolic Smoke Ball," 14 *J. Legal Stud.* 345, 372 (1985).

35. Id.

36. 15 U.S.C. §§2301–12.

37. 15 U.S.C. §2304.

38. U.C.C. §2-316.

39. U.C.C. §2-317(a).

40. See Writers' Guild of America, West, *Screen Credits Manual II.A.d.1*, available at http://www.wga.org/subpage_writersresources.aspx?id=170.

41. Id. For a case upholding these rules, see Ferguson v. Writers Guild of Am., W., Inc., 277 Cal. Rep. 450, 453 (Ct. App. 1991).

42. See Fed. Trade Comm'n, *Report on Automobile Warranties* 11 (1970).

43. See, e.g., Les Jackson, "Warranties Get Better with Cars," *Washington Times,* Jan. 16, 2004, at G10.

44. See FTC Unfair Credit Practices Rules, 16 C.F.R. §§444.1(i), 444.2(a)(4) (2005).

45. See Susan Lorde Martin & Nancy White Huckins, "Consumer Advocates vs. the Rent-to-Own Industry: Reaching a Reasonable Accommodation," 34 *Am. Bus. L.J.* 385 (1997). The abuse in this industry first came to light in an exposé in the *Wall Street Journal.* See Alix M. Freedman, "Peddling Dreams: A Marketing Giant Uses Its Sales Prowess to Profit on Poverty," *Wall Street Journal,* Sept. 22, 1993, at A1.

46. See 161 A.2d at 86.

47. See, e.g., Ian Ayres, "Menus Matter," 73 *U. Chi. L. Rev.* 3 (2006); Ian Ayres, "Regulating Opt Out: An Economic Theory of Altering Rules," 121 *Yale L.J.* 2032 (2012).

Epilogue

1. 333 P. 2d 757 (1958).

2. Id. at 760 (emphasis added).

3. 169 F.2d 684 (D.C. Cir. 1948).

4. 117 N.E. 807 (N.Y. 1917).

5. R. H. Coase, "The Problem of Social Cost," 3 *J.L. & Econ.* 1, 43 (1960).

6. Aristotle, *Nicomachean Ethics* 5.7.

INDEX

Alaska Packers' Association v. Domenico, 113–18
Allegheny College v. National Chautauqua County Bank, 32, 155
ambiguity, 20, 34–36, 66, 89
American Law Institute, 65
Anglo-American legal tradition, ix, 1, 39
anticipatory breach, 61–64
arbitration, 144
Aristotle, 151
Austin Instrument, Inc. v. Loral Corp., 121
Ayres, Ian, 145, 159, 166

"bad man" theory of contract, 46–47, 49–50
bankruptcy, in *Hamer v. Sidway*, 38, 39, 42, 44
bargained-for exchange: formal rules and, 36, 149; *Hamer v. Sidway* as, 29; legally enforceable promises and, 3, 26, 30–31, 39; *Mills v. Wyman* as, 34
bargaining, costless, as heuristic, 59, 60, 73, 94
bargaining power, contract law and, 133, 135
Benjamin, Judah P., 17–18, 19, 21
"Big Boy" letters, 94
Blackstone, William, 13–14
break-up fees, 76
Brooklyn Bridge problem, 149
bust-up fees, 76

Cardozo, Benjamin, 32, 149
Carlill v. Carbolic Smoke Ball Co., 141–44
Carroll v. Bowersock, 107–8
cartels, 116, 135
casualty to identified goods, 11
charitable subscriptions, enforceability of, 33
Chicago Board of Trade, regulation of, 85
Coase, Ronald, ix, 60, 150
Coase theorem, 60
Coke, Lord, 26
Commentaries (Blackstone), 13–14
Common Law (Holmes), 2–3, 47, 58
compensatory sum, contractual duty as obligation to pay, 48, 50, 53, 58, 77
concilience, contract theory and, 50, 158
cons, big and short distinguished, 130
consensus ad idem, 13
consequential damages, 71–74, 135
consideration: contract enforceability and, 3, 26; as formal rule, 36, 41; modifications of contract and, 52, 112
contracts to arrive, 11–12
Corbin, Arthur, 30–33, 41, 65, 145
cross–collateralization clauses, 137–38
customs of the trade, 21–23, 77, 81, 94–95, 129

Death of Contract (Gilmore), 3, 4, 5, 11, 57–58, 147
De Cicco v. Schweitzer, 149
default rules, 7, 60, 76, 129, 159
demurrer, 10
disclaimers, 73, 93, 123
disclosure: duties of, 84–89; law merchant and 85; nondisclosure as misrepresentation, 89; postcontractual, 91–95; relationships of trust and, 90–91
Drennan v. Star Paving Co., 147–48
due process, 140
duress: accessibility of courthouse and, 117; consideration and, 112, 114, 120; judicial error and, 118–19, 121; Posner's theory of, 111–22; preliminary injunctions and, 117–19; situational monopoly and, 114, 117, 120
duty of the forthright negotiator, 20–21

Economic Analysis of Law (Posner), 58, 115
efficient breach, 58
Embry v. Hargadine-McKittrick Dry Goods Co., 4–6, 153
Epstein, Richard, ix, 54
excuse, 102–10
exempt property, fine print and, 137–39
expectation damages: as foundational principle of contract law, 3, 8; anticipatory breach and, 61–64; consequential damages and, 71–74; efficient breach and, 58; excuse and, 103–4, 110; hard edges of, 64–67; Holmes and, 64–65; internalization of harm and, 60–61; mistake and, 102; option pricing and, 74–77; overreliance and, 67–69; Posner and, 58–61; specific performance and, 61; spot price and, 61–64

Federal Rules of Civil Procedure, 10
Fibrosa Spolka Akcyjna v. Fairbairn L.C.B. Ltd., 107, 162

fine print: criminal sanctions and, 123; product attribute, 124–27; signal dampening, 143–44
Flower City Painting Contractors v. Gumina Construction, 20–21, 65–66, 154
formal legal rules: cautionary function, 137; family relationships and, 44; weaknesses of, 23, 44
forum-selection clauses, 125, 144
forward contract, 11–12, 61–62
fraudulent conveyance, *Hamer v. Sidway* and, 38, 39
Friendly, Henry, 19–20
Frigaliment Importing Co. v. B.N.S. International Sales Corp., 19–20, 154
Fuller, Lon, 137
futures contract, 11–12, 61–62

Gilmore, Grant, 3–4, 15, 21, 57–58, 147
Globe Refining Co. v. Landa Cotton Oil Co., 7, 73, 153
good faith: definition of, 8, 78–84; disclosure and, 92–94; fraud and, 82; inquiry notice and, 81; postcontractual, 91–95
Goodman v. Dicker, 148–49

Hadley v. Baxendale, 70–74
Hamer, Louise, 37, 43, 45
Hamer v. Sidway, 7, 25–45, 65
Hand, Learned (judge), 17, 18
Harriman, Edward Avery, 47–56
Harvard Law School, 2, 25–26
Henningsen v. Bloomfield Motors, Inc., 124, 133–36, 144–45
Hippocrates, 34
Holmes, Oliver Wendell, Jr. (judge): consideration as bargained-for exchange, 26–27, 41; contract theory and, ix, 2, 3, 5; Posner and, 58; pragmatism and, 51; *Raffles v. Wichelhaus* and, 14–17, 19, 23
Holmes, Oliver Wendell, Sr. (poet), 2–3, 46, 153
hostage, exempt property as, 137

incompletely reasoned agreements, 44, 45, 156
information, disclosure of, 85–89
insurance, contract damages as, 49, 73, 132
interpretation of contracts, 19–23

Jackson, Thomas, ix
Jackson v. Seymour, 101
James, Henry, 149
James, William, 15, 49
judgment on the pleadings, 10
juries: fine print and, 135, 142; good faith and 82, 83, 90, 93; imperfect fact finding and, 5, 18, 40, 74

Kenobi, Obi-Wan, 79
Kessler, Fritz (Friedrich), 145

Laidlaw v. Organ, 84–86, 90, 101
Langdell, Christopher Columbus, 2, 5, 150
last-clear chance, 101
law merchant, 14, 85, 123
Lingenfelder v. Wainwright Brewing Co., 51–52
Llewellyn, Karl, 81

Magnuson-Moss Warranty Act, 143
markets: liquidity of, 86–87; manipulation of, 88; regulation of, 78, 85
Market Street Associates Ltd. Partnership v. Frey, 91–95, 111, 161
Marshall, John (Chief Justice), 85, 90
meeting of the minds, 3, 14–16, 20–21
merchants: contract law and, 1; customs of, 78–79, 129–30; fair dealing and, 81, 129; norms of, 22–23, 81, 129–30
Mills v. Wyman, 33–36, 42
misrepresentation, 79, 85, 89, 99, 129, 132, 148
Missouri Furnace Co. v. Cochrane, 61–64
mistake: expectation damages and, 102; mutual, 96–100; unilateral, 101–2
mitigation, duty of, 71, 104, 110

negligence, 48, 57, 72, 101, 108, 148
Norris-LaGuardia Act, 120
notarized documents, as formal legal rule, 44

objective intent, contract formation and, 3, 15–19
Opera Company of Boston v. Wolf Trap, 104–10
option, performance of promise as, 52, 55, 77
Oxxford Clothes XX v. Expeditors International of Washington, Inc., 112–13, 116–19

paternalism, fine print and, 136–40
Path of the Law (Holmes), 46–56
Peerless, 9–13, 19, 96
penalty clauses, rationale for, 76–77
penalty defaults, 71–72
Pierce, Charles Sanders, 15, 49
Posner, Richard: duress and, 111–22; efficient breach and, 58; good faith and, 91–95, 111; Holmes's heir, 57; influence of, ix
pragmatism, 14, 48–51, 119
precedent, 2
preliminary injunction, availability of and expectation damages, 117–19
primary obligation to perform, contractual duty as, 49, 50, 51–55
promises, enforceability of, 1, 25
promissory estoppel, 5, 26, 32
proper names, contract interpretation and, 15–17, 22

quasi-contract, 65

Raffles v. Wichelhaus, 7, 9–13, 19, 96
reformation of contracts, 96
reliance damages: alternatives to, 41; as basis for enforcing promises, 5, 31, 36; excuse and, 108; imperfect fact finding and, 40; overreliance and, 69–70; promissory estoppel and, 65, 147–49
renegotiation, of contracts, 75, 111

repose, 100–2
reputation, contract law and, 22, 77, 127, 129, 130, 159
Restatement (Second) of Contracts, 33, 99–100
Restatement of Torts, 89
rights-based conception of law, 45, 146
Roman law, 14

Savigny, Friedrich Carl von, 14
Schwartz, Alan, 145
Scott, Robert, ix
sealing wax, as formal rule, 6
Sears, Richard, 124
SEC v. Texas Gulf Sulfur Co., 86, 160
Sherwood v. Walker, 96–100
short cons, fine art of, 130–33
Sidway, Franklin, 36–37, 43
Simpson, A.W. Brian, ix, 9–13, 19, 141, 154, 165
social promises, enforceability of, 25–26, 40
specific relief: availability of, 51, 55, 56, 61; incentives of, 76
spot price, expectation damages and, 61–64
standardized terms, mass markets and, 125, 133–34
Story, James, 41–43, 44

Story, Joseph (Justice), 81
Story, William: character of, 41; nieces as heirs, 42, 43; promise to nephew, 25–26; relationship with brother, 42–43, 44
Sutton, Willie, 130
Swift v. Tyson, 79–84

tacit-agreement test, 7, 73
Taylor v. Caldwell, 104
tort: damages and, 60, 72; last-clear chance, 101; relationship with contract, 5, 48, 54, 149
tortious interference with contract, 54–55
trade usage, 21–24
Traynor, Roger (Justice), 147–48
trusts and estates, contract law and, 44

waivers, 133, 137–39
warranties, 97, 125–27, 129, 132, 134, 143–44
Williams v. Walker-Thomas Furniture Co., 124, 137–39, 144–45
Williston, Samuel, 29–31, 65

Yale Law School, 30, 145
Young Astronomer, 2, 14–15, 29, 46, 50, 56, 119, 121